A Complete Guide
for Players, Parents, and Coaches

P. Nerenberg, MSc, RD and M. Lacoste, BSc (FSc)

THE NUTRITION EDGE FOR HOCKEY PERFORMANCE
third edition

Published by Margot van Wettum-Lacoste and Pearle Nerenberg
Montreal, Quebec
www.eatthisforperformance.com

ISBN 978-0-9921681-3-1

Graphic Design & Production of the first edition: Tammy Desnoyears, www.tammydesign.ca
Graphic design update: Sebrina Jones & Rooha Janjua Conversion to ebook: www.gloryepublishingservices.com
Editor of the first edition: Brian Scrivener, www.scrivenerediting.com
Editor of the third edition: Asher Gray, www.aagray.com
Reviewed by Martin Fréchette Dt.P. M.Sc., Sports Nutritionist, mfrechette.nutrition@gmail.com

Recipes and menus: www.SOSCuisine.com/hockey SOS CUISINE.com®

Photo credits: Natacha Silber Photography; Kathleen Girard, Studio Photo Cookie; Marcus Nerenberg
Unidentified players during the CSM Dunarea Galati vs CSS HSC Csikszereda game, November 17, 2012 in Galati, Romania. Copyright PhotoStock10 (How to Get The Edge), (Chapter 11);
Players of men's national junior ice hockey team during open training in Novogorsk training center, Moscow region, Russia on April 12, 2013. Copyright Lilyana Vynogradova Chapter 31
All other photos are used under license from Shutterstock unless otherwise stated.

WHY EVERY HOCKEY PLAYER SHOULD READ **EAT THIS FOR HOCKEY PERFORMANCE**

"As coaches, we devote much of our teaching process towards conditioning, fundamentals, team strategies, and the mental approach, all with the intention of maximizing performance. All of these elements hinge on one very important factor – how much gas is in our players' tanks?"

– Gordon Armstrong, Professional Hockey Coach and Technical Director

"Sports nutrition is a game changer that is not paid attention to early enough in a high performance hockey player's career. It is one of the final pieces of the puzzle between success and could have been."

– Mel Davidson, General Manager for Hockey Canada's Women's Program and two-time Olympic Gold Medal Head Coach.

"The Nutrition Edge is a great read. I found it to be informative and easy to understand. This book will help hockey players (young and old alike) to maximize their on-ice performance."

– Linda Staal, hockey mom to four NHL players.

About your Sports RD

PEARLE NERENBERG, MSc, Registered Dietitian, IOC and ISAK certified

PHOTO: NATACHA SILBER

Pearle Nerenberg is a registered dietitian with an expertise in sports nutrition and a member of the Professional Order of Dietitians of Quebec. She is the founder of Eat This for Performance, a nutrition consultation company that offers her active followers guidance. She launched a weekly broadcast in 2018 to bring tools, tips, and insights into the nutrition world of high performance to your inbox. She works with youth and professional hockey players and teams, like the Canadiennes de Montréal, a semi-professional women's team. She has worked with the NHL franchises, players in the Quebec Junior Major League, players in the NCAA, players in the CIS, and National Team calibre players. She brings her extensive knowledge of the game of hockey to this great resource as a former NCAA hockey player for Cornell University and current hockey coach for hockey players aged 6 to 18.

Acknowledgements

A great thank you to my family and my hockey family for believing in me and encouraging my dreams. With the support of my parents, Lys and Marcus, who drove me to every hockey arena in Quebec (and beyond) and who fed me a healthy diet before anything close to this book was available, I was able to become a successful hockey player.

This book is dedicated to Rachel, Liam, and Mark
– Pearle Nerenberg

About your Hockey Mom

MARGOT LACOSTE, BSc (Food Science)

PHOTO: KATHLEEN GIRARD, STUDIO PHOTO COOKIE

Margot Lacoste is a retired dietitian and hockey mom to four in Montreal, Quebec. Her experience raising children who play hockey, and advising hockey players and teams, led her to self-publish the first version of The Nutrition Edge for Hockey Players in 2002. She brings her expansive knowledge of hockey schedules, arenas, tournament schedules, and teenage hockey player preferences to this practical guide.

PHOTO: MARCUS NERENBERG

Acknowledgements

I would like to thank my family and friends whose encouragement and support have allowed me to spread The Nutrition Edge message to a wider audience. My husband, Pierre, has helped me to see hockey from a coach's perspective. My children Sophie, Nicolas, William and Elise, through their athletic successes, have reinforced my firm belief that nutrition is the key to getting the edge on the competition.

I would like to dedicate this book to my Dad, who was a great motivator and role model. He gave me the confidence to succeed in my career and was so proud of me. I miss him every day.

– Margot Lacoste

The authors would like to thank Martin Fréchette P.Dt. M.Sc., Sports Nutritionist, for reviewing and adapting the French version of The Nutrition Edge for Hockey Performance

Table of Contents

START HERE TO EAT 4 PERFORMANCE

THE NUTRITION EDGE IS THE ADVANTAGE A HOCKEY PLAYER WILL GET BY EATING THE RIGHT FOODS AT THE RIGHT TIME.

If you are a hockey player, use the information here to guide your nutrition habits. The best hockey players are practicing their nutrition habits right now. The more guidelines you follow from **Eat This for Performance in Hockey**, the bigger the advantage you will have over those hockey players who don't bother to find out more about how critical nutrition is to their on-ice performance.

There is a reason we show you the number 4 in this introduction. Here you will find 4 moments around hockey where food can shape your performance in this great game.

1. 3-4 hours before hockey
2. 1-2 hours before hockey
3. During hockey
4. After hockey

At each moment there is a precise arrangement of food that can optimally energize you for hockey.

1. **Complete Meals** 3-4 hours before hockey
2. **Energizer Snacks** 1-2 hours before hockey
3. **Quick Energizer** Snacks During hockey
4. **Muscle builders** + Energizers After hockey

Eat 4 Performance Hockey Programs

Eat This 4 Performance in Hockey programs will give you the understanding you need to get to the next level of hockey performance. In the programs you will combine the information you learn with actual recipes to get you going on a performance nutrition plan. You can already start cooking recipes from each of the 4 categories with the SOS Cuisine online menu planner. Find the recipes for hockey performance at www.soscuisine.com/hockey.

Go to: www.EatThisForPerformance.com/Hockey

Unsure of which chapters to start with? Take the hockey nutrition quiz now to see what chapters you should read first.

THE HOCKEY NUTRITION QUIZ

Circle your answer to these 6 questions.

1. To get energy for hockey, which item would you reach for first?	2. What is the one habit you think would be hardest to stick to?
a) vitamins b) bread c) broccoli d) coffee	a) eating breakfast every day b) eating less junk food c) eating 3 to 4 hours before a game d) eating a healthy lunch at school or work
3. What are you most curious about?	**4. On game day, how do you eat?**
a) having more energy b) how food digests c) growing muscles d) my body weight	a) I get something at the snack bar. b) I make sure I eat the family meal. c) I eat a meal and snacks if I'm hungry. d) Sometimes I don't eat much.

5. During a game, how long does your energy last?	6. Which one of these would you be most likely to do?
a) I usually feel low energy from the start.	a) have a cola drink during a game
b) I run out of energy by the third period.	b) eat french fries before a game
c) I mostly just run out of energy on tournament days.	c) eat a chocolate bar right after a game
d) My energy levels are mostly good but I would like to know how to make them even better.	d) drink a protein shake in between periods

THE KEY

Circle the answer you chose and put the corresponding chapter number in the box to the right.	The chapters you should read first:
Example a) 1 b) 18 c) 21 d) 8	Example Chapter: 18
1. a) 1 b) 3 c) 5 d) 28	Chapter:
2. a) 13 b) 17 c) 24 d) 26	Chapter:
3. a) 18 b) 24 c) 21 d) 19	Chapter:
4. a) 39 b) 24 c) 30 d) 24	Chapter:
5. a) 37 b) 31 c) 36 d) 38	Chapter:
6. a) 33 b) 24 c) 34 d) 31	Chapter:

Getting The nutrition edge is easy if everyone — players, parents, teammates, and coaches — contributes. Players, you need to take responsibility for what you eat. Parents, you need to make sure that there are plenty of healthy foods available at home. Parents, coaches, and teammates should encourage good habits, not only by what they say, but also by what they do. We wrote this book so that you can help yourself.

EDITORIAL CREDIT: ©PHOTOSTOCK10

There are many different ways that you can get something out of this book:

- Flip through the book, look at the pictures, and read the little informative text boxes. You can learn a lot from them.
- Look at the Table of Contents and decide which chapters interest you the most and read them first. There is a quick answer at the beginning of each chapter if you are in a real hurry.
- Read the book from cover to cover. It's organized in a way that helps you gradually learn about making the best food choices. Re-read chapters that you really connect with.

Once you have read through some or all of the chapters, Dig Deeper into the section at the end of the book:

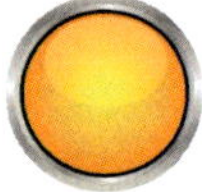

- Use the stoplight guides in the Digging Deeper Section to see what are your best sources of carbohydrates, fat, and protein.
- Compare what you eat to the sample menus in the Digging Deeper Section to see if you can make better food choices and improve the timing of your meals around games and practices.
- If you want to learn more about how labels can help you make the best food choices, check out Understanding the Canadian Nutrition Facts Label.
- Use the Digging Deeper Helpful Resources to explore other areas of nutrition that particularly interest you.
- Use the information in the Digging Deeper Section to make a hockey food kit to put in your hockey bag for excellent meals and snacks on the go.

As you can see, reading this book can be a little like playing hockey. There is a lot of back and forth, staying longer in some corners than others, and it takes time and practice to be good at it. So, what part of the book have you decided to look at first? Go ahead, jump in, and get the nutrition edge.

Have you ever read something or been told something about nutrition that sounded too good to be true or just plain wrong? Sometimes people hear things about nutrition and they repeat them to others without making sure that they are true. Parents, coaches, teachers, trainers, and even NHL players can make this mistake. Use this book and the other resources named in the Digging Deeper Section to make sure you are getting accurate advice before making any drastic change in your diet.

SECTION 1: The Basics

1. WHERE DOES ENERGY FOR HOCKEY COME FROM?

Quick Answer

Foods and drinks that have the special high-energy nutrients called carbohydrates and fats are the ones that will fill up your energy stores for hockey. Here we call them "Energizers". Smart hockey players know that whatever you eat and drink needs to be chewed, swallowed, and moved through the digestive system before it can even be absorbed into your body. Fill your energy stores for hockey by eating the energy nutrients, carbohydrates and fats, at the right time.

As a hockey player, you need to be able to work hard. All the sprinting and stopping that you do when you play hockey uses up a lot of energy. Fortunately, your body has built-in battery packs, much like a cell phone! Your battery packs are found in the cells of your muscles and liver. Like a cell phone, you can run out of energy in your battery packs. When you do not eat for many hours, your battery packs get low and you feel tired. This is because your body is actually missing energy. The goal of every hockey player is to time eating meals and snacks so that the battery packs are close to full when it comes time to play.

Unlike a cell phone, you cannot simply plug yourself in to get charged. Instead, you need to eat and move food and drink through your digestive system, a long muscular tube that runs from your mouth to your bottom. You need to have a healthy digestive system in order for your body to take the nutrients that it needs out of the food that you eat and to put them where they are useful in your body. How do you make sure that your digestive system is healthy? Work it out! There is no need to take your digestive system to the gym to work it out. By eating a lot of unprocessed foods (whole fruit, whole grains, and vegetables) and drinking a lot of water, you can keep your digestive muscles in top shape.

Once energy is absorbed into your body through your digestive system, it can be stored. Energy is stored by your body in two ways. One way is in the form of carbohydrates. You may have heard of food being full of carbs, but did you know your muscles are full of them too? The second way that energy can be stored is as fat. Not all fat is stored around your body where you can see it - some fat is actually stored in your muscles.

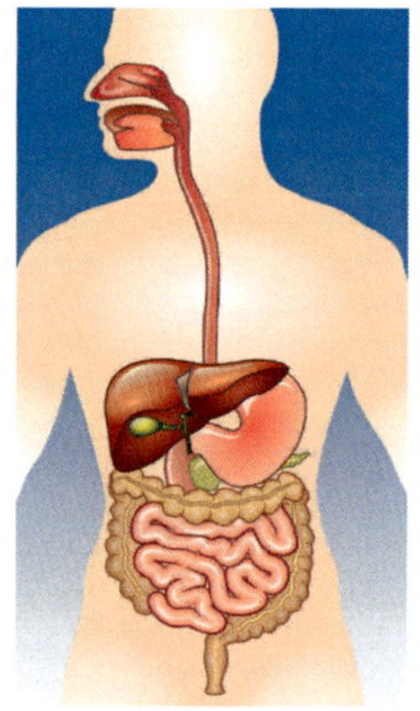

Does that mean you should eat carbohydrates and fat to have energy? Absolutely!

We like to call carbohydrates "Energizers" because they are the main source of energy for your muscles when you sprint. You find carbohydrates in foods and drinks that have starches or sugars. Starches come from grains (breads and cereals are some examples) or starchy vegetables (corn and potatoes are some examples). A starch is actually a bunch of sugars all stuck together like pearls on a string. When starches are chewed and swallowed, they split up and are absorbed by the body in the form of single sugars. So, if you eat a food with sugar (fruit and milk are some examples) you are eating a simpler form of carbohydrate.

Fat comes from foods with added fats and from foods that are mostly fat like butter, margarine, and avocados. If fat is not needed right away, it will be stored by your body. Be careful. You might be eating more fat than you need because fat is hidden in so many foods, especially foods that are sources of proteins, like meat, cheese, and nuts.

Understanding that a food has carbohydrates and fat is just the beginning. Read on to learn how to choose the right food at the right time.

Just because a food has carbohydrates and fats does not mean that it is necessarily good for you. You need to be a smart label reader to find out if the carbohydrates and fats in a food are the types that you want in the quantity that you want. In general, foods with a lot of added sugar or fat are not good choices.

WARNING

Nutrition Facts

Serving Size 1 Cup (53g/1.9 oz.)
Servings Per Container About 9

Amount Per Serving	
Calories 188	Calories from Fat 25
	% Daily Value*
Total Fat 3g	**5%**
Saturated Fat 0g	**0%**
Trans Fat 0g	
Cholesterol 0mg	**0%**
Sodium 80mg	**3%**
Potassium 300mg	**9%**
Total Carbohydrate 37g	**12%**
Dietary Fiber 8g	**32%**
Soluble Fiber	
Insoluble Fibe	**4%**
Sugars 13g	
Protein 9g	**14%**

2. WHY IS IT IMPORTANT TO EAT MORE THAN PASTA TO PLAY HOCKEY?

Quick Answer

Pasta is a great energizer, but pasta alone provides only some of the critical nutrients called protein, vitamins, and minerals that can help make a hockey player great. Your brain, muscles, and bones depend on all of these nutrients in the right amounts to get the nutrition edge. Without protein, vitamins, and minerals, your brain would not be able to tell your muscles to move, you would not have enough muscle mass to get out of bed, and your bones would break very easily.

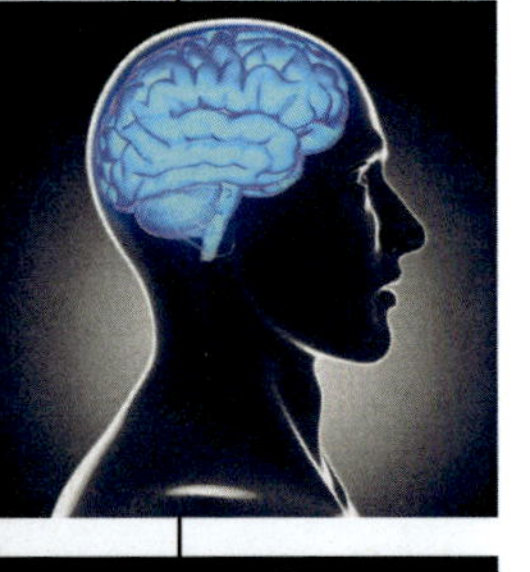

When you look at the best hockey players in the world, you will notice some similarities. For one, they are all muscular. However, there are some characteristics that you can't see that are just as important to on-ice performance as a muscular build. Like what, you ask? Well, how solid their bones are (high bone density) or the number of nerves that they have connecting their brain to their muscles.

Muscles cannot do all the work by themselves:

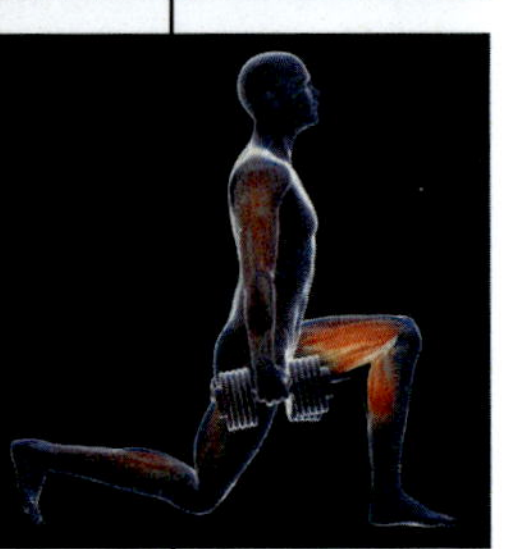

You need a strong signal to start in your brain and tell the right muscles to move. You can build strong signals by repeating the motions that you would like your muscles to do and by eating foods made of protein, vitamins, and minerals.

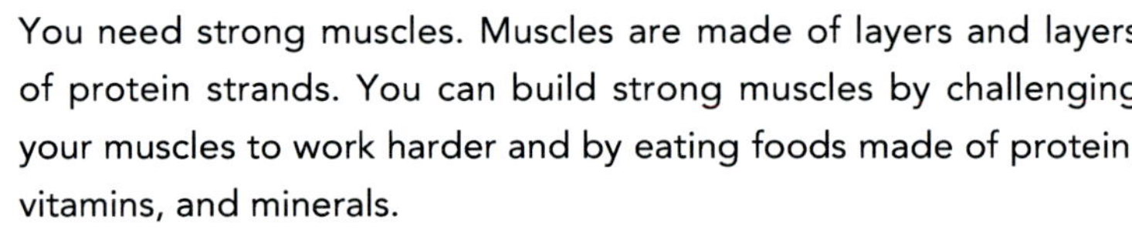

You need strong muscles. Muscles are made of layers and layers of protein strands. You can build strong muscles by challenging your muscles to work harder and by eating foods made of protein, vitamins, and minerals.

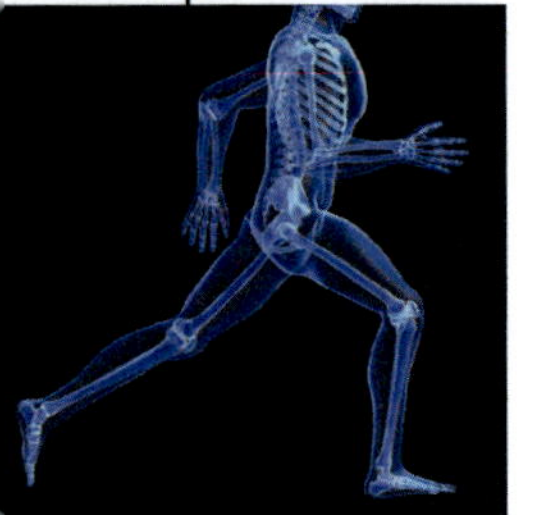

You need strong bones. You can build strong bones by doing high impact exercise and by eating foods made of protein, vitamins, and minerals.

Eating foods made of protein, vitamins, and minerals is really, really important for you to be able to use the energy in your body. The key thing to remember is that vitamins and minerals help you use energy, but they are not a source of energy. Confusing? If you understand the idea that your body can store energy like a cell phone, let's take it one step further with the idea that protein, vitamins, and minerals are like the apps on your cell phone. The battery packs in your phone give it energy. Apps don't give your cell phone energy, but they do make your cell phone do all the fun things you want it to do. By eating foods or drinks which contain more protein, vitamins, and minerals you will be making it possible for your body to use the energy you stored up.

Jamie's Story: "My best friend told me that professional hockey players all eat pasta before hockey, so I started to eat pasta as much as possible. One week I ate pasta almost every day, and sometimes I had pasta at lunch and supper. My parents thought I was eating too much pasta! I was so shocked when I found out that I felt better on the ice when I ate a mixture of pasta and turkey meat balls before my game. I thought that maybe the turkey meat balls are better than pasta! So, the next game I ate a ton of turkey meat balls and sauce and no pasta (I was a little sick of pasta), but during the game I felt like death, and I will never do that again! I realized I need to have both foods to feel good during my game."

TESTIMONIAL

3. WHAT IS A CALORIE?

Quick Answer

Calories can be a way of explaining how much energy is needed to play hockey. We can count the calories in a food, and we can count the calories needed to skate one length of the ice. To have enough energy for your game, you need to eat enough calories for all the skating you do. But be careful, if you just look at the calories in food you might forget that including foods with high nutrient value (foods that have protein, vitamins, and minerals as well as calories) will give you the nutrition edge.

Your body uses the calories from the food that you eat to give it the energy it needs to survive and to meet any extra demands placed upon it (such as growth spurts). You can use the words "energy" or "calories" and it will mean the same thing. As a hockey player, your body needs energy not only to move on the ice, but also to repair muscles and tissues. Chapter 1 explained that energy for hockey comes from carbohydrates and fats, so these two nutrients have calories. Protein has calories too. But, you should not rely on the calories in protein to give you energy to train and play hockey.

Some foods are loaded with calories, and some have next to none. You cannot tell by the number of calories whether or not a food is good for you. What you have to decide is whether or not you are getting good nutrient value for your calories. In the case of french fries, the answer would be no! In the case of a bowl of Cheerios®, the answer would be yes. To get the nutrition edge, make sure you get calories and nutrients from the foods you eat. The Digging Deeper Section will give you some great label-reading tips to help you figure out which foods are full of empty calories (a lot of calories, but not a lot of nutrients) and which foods provide you with nutrients along with the calories.

Here are examples of the number of calories found in certain foods and a comparison of the nutrient value of these foods:

FOOD OR DRINK	NUMBER OF CALORIES	NUTRIENT VALUE
1 small apple	60	Great!
290 ml of vitamin water	60	Poor!
1 slice of whole grain bread	90	Great!
1 slice of white bread	90	Poor!
2 1/3 cup (580ml) of Cheerios®	220	Great!
1 serving of french fries	220	Poor!

Source: Canadian Nutrient File 2010, rounded values

Sean's Story: "I heard that candy is packed full of empty calories, but I still like to eat it sometimes. I wasn't even sure what empty calories were until my Sports RD (Registered Dietitian) explained it to me. He said eating empty calories before a hockey game was like showing up to play a game with a bag full of only one type of hockey equipment such as a bag full of hockey gloves. Then I understood what empty calories meant. Even though that hockey bag is full of equipment, it might as well be empty because you can't play a hockey game with only gloves. He asked me what piece of hockey equipment I would want to have in my bag if I could only have one. Hmmm... skates I think. But the refs still wouldn't let anyone play a hockey game if they only had skates."

TESTIMONIAL

4. HOW MANY CALORIES DO I NEED?

Quick Answer

The more active you are, the more calories you need. Even if you are a real couch potato, your body still needs calories for its basic functions. Your calorie needs are not the same each day. As a growing hockey player, you will need more calories one day and less the next. There is no tool or computer program that can accurately tell you how many calories you need, so counting calories is not going to help you get the nutrition edge. Instead, when you feel hungry, eat foods high in good nutrients.

Even when you are sleeping, you need energy to keep your vital organs going - your heart, brain, kidneys, and lungs. Your body needs energy to remain at a normal temperature, to digest and absorb food, and to help you grow and develop. An adequate amount of calories from carbohydrates is crucial to your performance because your muscles need this energy to play hockey.

Your body uses the same amount of calories sleeping for 8 hours as it does playing 1 hour of hockey.

INFO

Professional NHL hockey players have been found to need between 2500 to 5000 calories per day. As a young hockey player, you may need 2000 to 4000 calories or more each day. The exact number depends on whether you are growing, how muscular you are, how much you weigh, and how active you are. Why is there such a big range? Because one day you might be resting and not doing any sports, and the next, you might have gym class plus an outdoor field trip at school and a hockey game at night. The more active you are, the more calories your body needs.

Sports nutrition scientists have not yet found a way to accurately measure the calorie needs of an individual hockey player. In fact, no one will be able to tell you how many calories you need just by looking at you. And, certainly no website or computer program will be able to accurately tell you how many calories you need. The only way to have a good idea of your calorie needs is to record the amounts of all foods and drinks you consume now and ask a professional Sports RD to evaluate your diet with you.

SPORTS RD SAYS:

Growth spurts can require a lot of extra calories. Often you will feel tired and hungry for more food than usual. Check your height often to see if you grew. You should consult a sports dietitian if you want to know:

- How many calories you need
- How to gain or lose weight
- Nutrition information or advice that is specific to YOU

If you are worried about gaining weight, keep in mind that teenagers should be gaining weight with every growth spurt. A growing teenager:

- Will lose weight or stay at the same weight if he or she eats fewer calories than his or her body needs. This is because the body of a growing person needs enough extra calories to be able to grow and develop.
- Will gain weight if he or she eats enough calories.
- Will gain excessive weight if he or she eats more calories than what is needed for normal weight gain associated with growth.

Counting calories will not help you. If you are overweight and don't want to gain too much weight as you grow, you need to be extra sure that the foods that you eat are very nutritious. That means staying away from soft drinks, chips, cookies, and cakes that only give your body calories, but very few nutrients. It is more important to consider where you are getting your calories from, rather than the number of calories you eat. You may get lots and lots of calories from foods like chocolate bars, cakes, and chips, but they sure won't give your body very many important nutrients! You need to make sure that you are including foods that will give you a variety of starches, proteins, vitamins, and minerals. You can find the right foods to eat in the Performance Foods List.

This way, you are sure that your body is not only getting the calories it needs, but also getting the nutrition edge.

5. WHY ARE CARBOHYDRATES SO IMPORTANT?

Quick Answer

Carbohydrates are the major fuel your body needs to play hockey. If your diet is low in carbohydrates, your hockey performance will suffer. Eat sources of carbohydrates from unprocessed starches and fruit instead of sources that have lots of sugar or refined grains.

The amount of carbohydrate stored in your body determines how long you can do any physical exercise. It's simple: if you don't get enough carbohydrate in your diet, your hockey performance will suffer because your muscles will run out of fuel.

You eat carbohydrates as either starches (grains or starchy vegetables like potatoes and corn) or sugars (found in many foods such as fruit, vegetables, milk, yogurt, and also in foods with added sugar). We like to call these types of carbohydrates "Energizers".

FIBRE - Even though it isn't digested and absorbed by your body (so it doesn't give your body calories or energy), fibre plays an important role in keeping your digestive tract healthy. It keeps your bowel movements regular and slows the digestion of food (making it easier for your body to absorb important nutrients). Fibre is found in plant foods. The best sources are vegetables, beans, oat products, psyllium and whole grain breads and cereals. Fibre can also be referred to as roughage or bulk.

DEFINITION

There is a third way you can eat carbohydrates: as fibre (broccoli, salad, bran flakes are some examples). Fibre is necessary to eat to keep your digestive system in top shape. However, high fibre foods take longer to digest than lower fiber foods so you need to give your body enough time to digest them before hockey. Don't eat high fiber foods right before hockey.

After the carbohydrates that you eat are digested, your body transports them in your blood and stores them in your liver and muscles. If you don't get enough carbohydrate in your diet, you won't have enough stored in your liver and muscles to do the work you need to do later.

You need to eat high-quality carbohydrates like fresh fruits and whole grains, rather than foods that have sugar added to them to make them sweeter, or foods that are highly processed. Foods with a lot of added sugar will provide your muscles with carbohydrate, but they have some disadvantages:

- The extra sugar calories will fill you up and you will have less room for more nutritious foods.
- They are really bad for your teeth.
- They can cause your blood sugar to rise up too high at first, then fall too low afterwards when your body tries to cope with the sugar load.

There is often confusion about brown sugar, honey, agave, and maple syrup. People think that they are a lot more nutritious than refined white sugar because they are naturally occurring sugars. The truth is that refined white sugar has no vitamins and minerals to speak of, and anything is better. Brown sugar, honey, agave, and maple syrup have slightly more vitamins and minerals than refined white sugar, but they are still pretty much pure sugar.

SPORTS RD SAYS: ***Hypoglycemia is a scientific way of saying not enough sugar in your blood. You can get hypoglycemia from not eating enough calories. You can also get it from eating too much sugar. But how can that be? If you eat a lot of sugar, how can you be missing sugar in your blood? A very good question! Well, when you eat a lot of sugar, it is digested very quickly and comes rushing into your blood. Your body is not happy to have too much sugar all of a sudden in your blood, so it fights back by quickly pumping a hormone that makes the sugar go out of your blood and into your muscles. Sometimes your body puts too much of the hormone in your blood, and this hormone keeps working even after your blood sugar level is normal. Oops. Then you get hypoglycemia.***

6. WHY DO I NEED PROTEIN?

Quick Answer

You need protein for the growth, maintenance, and repair of muscles and other tissues. We call foods rich in protein the "Muscle Builders". You need protein to grow hair and fingernails, produce hormones, replace red blood cells, and boost your immune system. Your protein needs can easily be met by eating a balanced diet.

Like carbohydrates, protein is a very important nutrient for athletes.

- You need protein to form muscles so that you can move.
- You need protein to make hormones to tell your muscles to move.
- You need protein to make enzymes that can break down food so you can get the energy you need to move.

AMINO ACIDS - Amino acids are the building blocks of protein. Your body can make some amino acids (non-essential) and not others (essential). Your body needs both types of amino acids, but you must get the essential amino acids from the foods that you eat. Proteins from animal sources (meat, fish, eggs, milk) have all of the essential amino acids. Proteins from plant sources (like beans, lentils, rice, tofu) are lacking in some essential amino acids, but you can make up for it by eating different protein sources throughout the day. For example, have rice with lentils at one meal and peanut butter and toast at the next meal.

DEFINITION

Protein is so important to movement that a hockey player should be eating some protein at every meal.

Protein comes from animal sources and plant sources. Animal proteins are found in meats, fish, seafood, dairy products, and eggs. Plant proteins are found in beans, peas, legumes, nuts, seeds, and grains. It is easy to get all the protein you need as an athlete by eating a variety of the plant and animal sources of protein at each meal.

Without protein your body could become weak, including your immune system, your hair, your fingernails, and, of course, your muscles. Luckily, it is easy to get all the protein you need by eating a balanced diet.

It is a myth that eating extra protein will build muscle. Exercise builds muscle, not extra protein. By eating enough calories and by making sure that some of your calories come from protein, your body will be able to use the protein in your diet to build muscle if you are strength training.

Do not fall into the trap of eating too much protein! Too much protein in a diet can be bad for you for the following reasons:

- Foods that are high in protein are often high in fat, so you may be getting too much fat in your diet if you eat too much protein.
- When you eat too much protein, it will either be burned for energy (not a very efficient process) or can be stored as fat.

SPORTS RD SAYS: ***Supplements and protein powders are a last resort for hockey players to meet their protein needs. With proper planning, hockey players can get all the protein they need from eating whole foods high in protein. For example, a 200 pound player like Sydney Crosby would get all the protein he needs in a day from:*** 2 slices of bread, a plate of pasta, 2 cups of rice, 2 granola bars, 500ml of milk, 2 eggs, 1 chicken breast, 1 bowl of yogurt, and 1 filet of fish.

7. IS ALL FAT BAD?

Quick Answer

No, not all fat is bad. Fats have an important role to play in our bodies. They are a concentrated source of energy. Body fat helps to protect vital organs and acts as an insulator against the cold. Fats also help you to absorb the fat-soluble vitamins (A, D, E, and K). They are a source of essential fatty acids. Last, but not least, they add flavour and texture to foods.

Hockey players need fat in their diets each day. Don't be afraid of foods with fat in them since a healthy diet includes foods that have fat. Eating a moderate amount of fat does not make you fat, but eating too much fat can cause you to store fat. Keep in mind that you do not need to go out of your way to eat food with fat. Just by eating a variety of protein and carbohydrates you will likely be getting most of the fat you need. Add little amounts of nuts and oils to your day to get some healthy fats and you're right on track!

ESSENTIAL FATTY ACID - Essential fatty acids are fats that your body cannot make therefore must get from your diet. Omega-3 fats are an example of an essential fatty acid. Fatty acids are key to a strong immune system.

OMEGA-3 FATS - Omega-3 fats can't be made by your body, so you have to get them from your diet. They have been found to benefit some people with arthritis and asthma and they have been linked to protecting people from getting heart attacks. They are found in fatty fish, seafood, some vegetable oils, walnuts, flax seeds, soy products and omega-3 fortified eggs.

HYDROGENATED FATS - Hydrogenated fats are oils that have been altered to be solid at room temperature. They are found in some margarines, some peanut butters, shortening, and naturally in very very small quantities in many foods. Current studies show that eating too much of these types of fats can be bad for your health.

If you avoid eating foods with fat you could hurt your hockey performance. Fat has been proven to be an important way for athletes to get energy, especially on days when you have been very active. Foods with fat are needed to absorb vitamins A, E, D, and K. These vitamins keep every part of your body healthy. Hockey players should eat more of the good fats.

ADD LITTLE AMOUNTS OF NUTS AND OILS TO YOUR DAY TO GET SOME HEALTHY FATS AND YOU'RE RIGHT ON TRACK!

When people talk about bad fats they are referring to saturated fats and trans fats. A bad fat would only be called bad if it does something horrible. Well, diets that are high in saturated fats and trans fat have been linked with causing heart disease, which is life-threatening. It takes many years (even decades) to develop heart disease, but the good habits to avoid this disease start young. Replacing your saturated fat intake with polyunsaturated fats and eliminating trans fats are habits you can start now. Saturated fats come mostly from animal products like meats, butter, and dairy products (except from dairy products made from skim milk). They can also be found in palm and coconut oils. Trans fats are found in fried foods (like doughnuts and french fries) and baked goods (like cakes, pies and cookies).

When people talk about good fats they are referring to polyunsaturated fats and monounsaturated fats. These fats are found in nuts, seeds, oils, and non-hydrogenated margarines. They are also found in fatty fish: salmon, trout, arctic char, herring, mackerel, sardines, and anchovies. You may have heard about omega-3 fatty acids. These are polyunsaturated fats that help to improve your body's functions.

GOOD FATS

SECTION 1

Polyunsaturated, monounsaturated, non-hydrogenated... Whew! That is a lot of complex words just to say this: Eat some nuts, seeds, and and oils every day (2 to 3 tablespoons, or 30 to 45 ml), and fatty fish two times a week.

Remember, too much of any type of fat in your diet is not good. High fat intake can cause you to gain weight, which definitely hinders your on-ice performance. The key to eating for a top performance is to eat small amounts of good fats every day.

Avoid fat free diets. They make it impossible for you to absorb certain vitamins.

FAT SOLUBLE VITAMINS - Vitamins A, D, E and K are fat-soluble vitamins. You don't need these vitamins every day because they are stored in your liver and fat tissues. These vitamins can be toxic if taken in large amounts, so be very careful if you are taking a supplement with only these vitamins.

WATER SOLUBLE VITAMINS - Vitamin C, the B vitamins (riboflavin, niacin, thiamin, pyridoxin, cobalamin, biotin and folic acid) are water-soluble vitamins. These vitamins can be lost easily by cooking in water, so be careful not to overcook and try to use the leftover cooking water in sauces and gravies. You need to eat foods with these vitamins every day because your body can't store them. If you get more than you need in a day, your body will just pee them out. If you get the extra vitamins from supplements, you will have very expensive urine!

DEFINITION

8. DO I NEED A MULTIVITAMIN?

Quick Answer

You do not need to take a multivitamin if you eat well. Eat a variety of good foods each day to get the essential vitamins and minerals that you need. Multivitamins are not recommended or needed for athletic performance or growth. If a professional assesses that your diet is missing a vitamin or a mineral, you will be encouraged to eat more foods containing those nutrients, and a single vitamin or mineral may be prescribed.

The majority of people do not need a multivitamin supplement. While vitamins and minerals are extremely important to your body, you only need them in small amounts each day. If you eat a variety of foods every day, especially fruit, vegetables and whole grains, you will meet your vitamin and mineral requirements.

If a dietitian determines that you are missing a specific vitamin or mineral in your diet, you will be given a list of foods that will help you to increase your intake of that specific nutrient, and you may be asked to take a supplement of that specific nutrient. Taking a multivitamin is unnecessary for most people.

The most common deficiencies in young athletes are Vitamin D, Calcium, Vitamin B6, Folate, and Iron. Just because these are the most common deficiencies does not mean that you are deficient in these nutrients. A blood test is normally needed to confirm deficiency.

Is it possible to take too many vitamins and minerals? Definitely. Taking too many vitamins and minerals can decrease your performance. Do not fall into the trap of thinking that more is better. More is not better when it comes to vitamins and minerals.

So, how do you know if you are getting what you need? Follow the guidelines in this book and eat vitamin- and mineral-rich foods as often as possible. A good intake of Superfoods **will help you get most of your vitamins and minerals.**

VITAMINS

VITAMIN D

Vitamin D helps your body to absorb and use calcium and phosphorus, which are needed for strong bones and teeth. Vitamin D can also protect you against infections by keeping your immune system healthy.

Vitamin D is not found naturally in many foods. In North America, foods such as milk, margarine, some soy or rice beverages and yogourts have vitamin D added to them. Good food sources of vitamin D include certain kinds of fish, egg yolks, and milk. There is a substance in your skin that turns into vitamin D when it is exposed to the sun. So, the sun is actually a source of vitamin D: 15 to 20 minutes of direct sun exposure (without sun-screen) to your arms, hands, and face will be enough to get your daily vitamin D dose. Be careful not to get too much sun, as too much sun exposure can be harmful.

FOLATE (FOLACIN OR FOLIC ACID)

This vitamin cannot be stored in your body, so you should eat folate-rich foods every day. Folate helps make red blood cells. If you do not have enough folate you may feel tired, weak, and unable to concentrate.

Dark green vegetables like broccoli and spinach and dried legumes such as chickpeas, beans, and lentils are naturally good sources of folate. In North America, folic acid is added to all white flour and enriched grain products.

VITAMIN B6 (PYRIDOXINE)

Your body uses Vitamin B6 to make and use protein and carbohydrates. Vitamin B6 is also needed to make working red blood cells so they can carry oxygen in your blood to your muscles.

The best sources of vitamin B6 include meat, fish, poultry, enriched cereals, soy products, nuts, lentils, and some vegetables (like potatoes, sweet potatoes, carrots) and fruits (like bananas and prunes).

MINERALS

CALCIUM

Calcium is a mineral that helps you build and maintain strong bones and teeth. Weak bones can break more easily than strong bones. Calcium is also needed to help your muscles move and your heart beat.

Milk, cheese, and milk alternatives like soymilk are excellent sources of calcium. Other sources include green, leafy vegetables (like spinach, kale, and swiss chard), canned fish, and tofu.

IRON

Iron is the part of red blood cells that carries oxygen around your body. You are considered anaemic if you have low blood iron levels. Low iron levels can leave you tired, pale looking, and irritable.

You can find iron in both animal and plant foods:

Animal sources include meat, fish, and poultry. Our bodies easily absorb this type of iron.

Plant sources include dried beans, peas and lentils, and some fruits and vegetables.

In North America, grain products like flour, pasta, and breakfast cereals are fortified with iron. Our bodies are better able to absorb plant and supplement iron when it is combined with meat/chicken/fish or a source of vitamin C. Vitamin C rich foods include citrus fruits and juices, cantaloupe, strawberries, broccoli, tomatoes, and peppers.

POTASSIUM (AN ELECTROLYTE)

Your heart needs potassium for it to work. Potassium is also needed for your muscles to contract. Athletes may need to replenish their potassium after a particularly long and sweaty workout.

Many foods contain potassium, including all meats, some types of fish (salmon, cod, and flounder), and many fruits (bananas, raisins, and oranges), vegetables (tomatoes, potatoes, spinach), and legumes. Dairy products are also good sources of potassium.

MAGNESIUM (AN ELECTROLYTE)

Magnesium helps you to use the energy from food, and it helps make new proteins. Magnesium is an important part of your bones and helps keep your muscles and nerves healthy.

The best sources of magnesium are legumes, nuts (almonds, peanuts, and cashews), spinach, fish, and whole grains.

SODIUM (THE MOST IMPORTANT ELECTROLYTE!)

Your body uses sodium to control your blood pressure, your muscle contractions, and to balance your body water. Most people consume way too much sodium and do not have to worry about getting enough in their diets. However, active people like hockey players are different. After a long hockey practice or game, you will need to replenish the sodium that you have sweated out.

How do you replenish your body's sodium? Have a source of sodium. Tomato juice, soup, cheese or a meal that includes food with added salt are high in sodium. Sports drinks are moderate sources of sodium.

SPORTS RD SAYS: ***A food with more vitamins and minerals added to it is not always better. Try getting your vitamins and minerals from nature's multivitamins: vegetables.***

9. WHY IS WATER SO GOOD TO DRINK?

Quick Answer

In one hockey game, you might lose about a kilogram (2 to 3 pounds) of water. You use water to control the temperature of your body. When you are hot, you lose more water than when you are cool. When you don't drink enough water, your body becomes dehydrated. Your on-ice performance will suffer if you are dehydrated.

It is really quite simple; you need water to replace the water you lose. You lose water mainly by breathing, peeing, and sweating. Diarrhea and vomiting can cause your body to lose a lot of water in a short period of time, so you have to make sure that you get enough liquid when you are sick.

If you lose too much water, you become dehydrated. Unfortunately, hockey players do not always recognize all the symptoms of dehydration and have unknowingly played entire games while dehydrated.

PHOTO: NATACHA SILBER

What are the symptoms of dehydration? A dry mouth is a common one. But did you know that muscle cramps, nausea, decreased sweating, and lightheadedness are also symptoms of dehydration? If avoiding these symptoms isn't enough to convince you to drink water regularly, then there is one bigger problem you should consider: low energy from dehydration. Even if you eat perfectly and train perfectly for hockey, if you do not hydrate your body well, you will not be able to play properly or recuperate quickly. Hockey players can start to feel low energy when they are dehydrated because their body is taking more time to recover from exertion.

ONE WAY TO STAY HYDRATED IS TO DRINK OFTEN ENOUGH IN THE DAY TO AVOID HAVING A DRY MOUTH.

So, how much should you drink? Well, everyone is different and there isn't one right answer for each person. One way to stay hydrated is to drink often enough in the day to avoid having a dry mouth. Some people may tell you to look at the colour of your pee. But your pee is not always a good test of your level of hydration. For instance, if you were dehydrated before a game and you chugged a bottle of water, your pee would become clear. However, the water you just chugged has gone into your body and out of your body and it has not had enough time to hydrate your body for your game.

SPORTS RD SAYS: ***If you want individual information about how much water you need to rehydrate yourself, work with a sports dietitian to get your dehydration rate assessed.***
www.eatthisforperformance.com/services

10. WHAT IS THE RIGHT AMOUNT OF CARBOHYDRATES, PROTEIN AND FAT TO EAT?

Quick Answer

The amount of carbohydrates, protein, and fat a hockey player should eat is very individual and based on many factors including how much muscle they have and how much they move. The more muscle weight hockey players have and the more they move, the more they need to eat. Hockey players don't need to count grams of carbs, protein, and fat. Eat a balanced plate we call the Hockey Player's Plate, listen to hunger cues, and eat regularly throughout the day to eat the right amount to have the nutrition edge.

HOCKEY PLAYER'S PLATE

Calculating the right amount of carbohydrates, protein, and fat you need involves several steps and professional guidance. The math calculations that sports dietitians use are based on your activity level on a specific day and based on your muscle, fat, and bone weight. The formulas used take years of training to master. To give you a sneak peak of what it takes to make a plan for a hockey player, check out Kevin's example plan for his carbohydrate needs. Don't follow Kevin's plan though, because it almost certainly will not be right for you - plus it is missing his requirements for protein and fat.

Kevin consults a sports dietitian to know how much carbohydrate he needs on the day he plays in a one-hour hockey qame:

SPORTS RD SAYS:

1. First, the sports dietitian might measure his body composition (amount of muscle, bone, and fat) using highly specialized expensive equipment. Let's say that Kevin has 63 kg (140 pounds) of muscle, fat and bone.

2. Second, the sports dietitian will multiply his weight in kilograms by a gram amount of carbohydrate needed for that particular day. The calculation for carbohydrate on Kevin's game day might be: 5 grams x 63 kilograms, which would be 315 grams.

3. Third, the sports dietitian will make a food plan that shows Kevin how much food equals 315 grams of carbohydrate.

a) 500ml milk
b) 2 slices of bread
c) 1 banana
d) 2 granola bars
e) 2 cups of cooked pasta
f) 175g of fruit yogurt
g) 2 cups of cooked rice
h) 1 cup of strawberries

Luckily you don't need to get your calculator to figure out how much carbohydrate, protein, and fat you need to eat -there is an easier way.

Look at the general pattern of what you eat. The emphasis should be on carbohydrates. A meal that includes a big steak and fries is not the balance that you are looking for (too much protein and fat!). It would be better to eat a smaller steak, with a baked potato and a salad. Piling sour cream or butter on your baked potato and dressing on your salad will also upset this balance. Hockey players should aim to make the proportions of the food on their plate look like the Hockey Player's Plate at each meal.

The Hockey Player's Plate is muscle builders (chicken, lean beef, tofu, etc.), energizers (pasta, rice, potatoes, etc.), and 1/3 colourful superfoods (carrots, sweet peppers, zucchini, etc.) Small amounts of dressings or sauces can be added to meals. If a light meal is needed because you are too close to hitting the ice, then eat less muscle builders and superfoods (keep the energizers the same). This meal is called the Light Hockey Player's Plate.

LIGHT HOCKEY PLAYER'S PLATE

Of course, breakfast and snacks can look different. You may be eating more fruit than vegetables at those times. It's good to know that fruit are energizer superfoods, meaning they offer a source of carbohydrate energy as well as other super nutrients.

Try to eat meals and snacks throughout the day. Your body will be using energy at all times. By eating regularly, you will be sure to stay energized. If you go more than five hours during the day without eating, you will probably start to feel really hungry - but this hunger signal comes too late for two reasons. One, when you are too hungry, it becomes harder to stop yourself from eating the wrong foods and overeating. Two, your body has been deprived of some key nutrients that are needed to build muscle and recover from a practice or game.

The more you exercise, the less you will be able to rely on your hunger cues. Make sure to eat every 2 to 4 hours whether your stomach rumbles or not.

Some people will try to tell you to avoid carbohydrates because they make you fat. The truth is that too many calories from either carbohydrates, protein, or fat can make you gain weight. It is the surplus or deficit of calories from any of these sources that decides whether you gain, maintain, or lose weight.

11. WHY ARE FOOD GUIDES HELPFUL?

Quick Answer

Food guides are great for translating complicated nutrient recommendations into real and understandable food choices. Many countries have their own food guides, based on the foods that are available locally and the food habits of the local people. In **Eat This for Performance in Hockey** we give you a **Performance Foods List** to target eating from every day. The 3 categories to eat from are Energizers, Muscle Builders, and Superfoods.

Extensive nutrition research has been done all over the world to determine what people need to eat in order to be healthy and well nourished. This international research has resulted in a long list of nutrients with recommended amounts needed for all people in each age group. Unless you are a nutrition expert (like a dietitian), you can't take this list to the grocery store and use it to buy nutritious food. What would you buy to give you 4 mg of pantothenic acid? Is the folate in the canned goods aisle? Most people would have no idea. That is where food guides come in handy. Food guides take all of the research behind the nutrient list and translate it into servings of real food that real people can understand.

If you go on the internet, you can find food guides from countries all over the world. They are all quite colourful and interesting to look at and come in many different shapes and sizes. A circle, a wheel, a plate, a pyramid, a rainbow, a pagoda, a compass, a house, and blocks are some of the shapes that you will see.

The Performance Foods List (PFL)

How to use the PFL: Choose the foods you like to eat from each category. Make meals from the energizers + muscle builders + superfoods. Make energizing snacks from energizers and filling snacks from superfoods or muscle builders. Keep in-play energizers for times when you need the extra energy right before, during, or right after your sport. The +'s mean there are significant amounts of hidden fats in that food. Fat is slow to digest so eating large amounts before hockey is not a good idea.

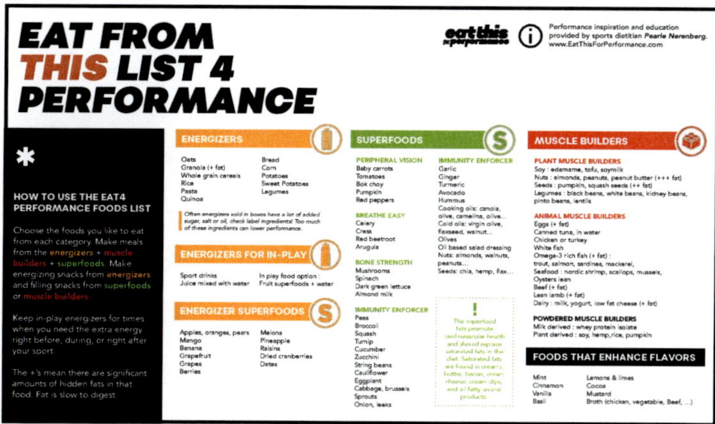

EAT FROM THIS LIST 4 PERFORMANCE

eat this 4 performance — Performance inspiration and education provided by sports dietitian ***Pearle Nerenberg.*** www.EatThisForPerformance.com

HOW TO USE THE EAT4 PERFORMANCE FOODS LIST

Choose the foods you like to eat from each category. Make meals from the energizers + muscle builders + superfoods. Make energizing snacks from energizers and filling snacks from superfoods or muscle builders.

Keep in-play energizers for times when you need the extra energy right before, during, or right after your sport.

The +'s mean there are significant amounts of hidden fats in that food. Fat is slow to digest.

ENERGIZERS

Oats
Granola (+ fat)
Whole grain cereals
Rice
Pasta
Quinoa
Bread
Corn
Potatoes
Sweet Potatoes
Legumes

Often energizers sold in boxes have a lot of added sugar, salt or oil, check label ingredients! Too much of these ingredients can lower performance.

ENERGIZERS FOR IN-PLAY

Sport drinks
Juice mixed with water
In play food option : Fruit superfoods + water

ENERGIZER SUPERFOODS

Apples, oranges, pears
Mango
Banana
Grapefruit
Grapes
Berries
Melons
Pineapple
Raisins
Dried cranberries
Dates

SUPERFOODS

PERIPHERAL VISION
Baby carrots
Tomatoes
Bok choy
Pumpkin
Red peppers

BREATHE EASY
Celery
Cress
Red beetroot
Arugula

BONE STRENGTH
Mushrooms
Spinach
Dark green lettuce
Almond milk

IMMUNITY ENFORCER
Peas
Broccoli
Squash
Turnip
Cucumber
Zucchini
String beans
Cauliflower
Eggplant
Cabbage, brussels
Sprouts
Onion, leeks

IMMUNITY ENFORCER
Garlic
Ginger
Turmeric
Avocado
Hummus
Cooking oils: canola, olive, camelina, olive...
Cold oils: virgin olive, flaxseed, walnut...
Olives
Oil based salad dressing
Nuts: almonds, walnuts, peanuts...
Seeds: chia, hemp, flax...

! The superfood fats promote cardiovascular health and should replace saturated fats in the diet. Saturated fats are found in creams, butter, bacon, cream cheese, cream dips, and all fatty animal products.

MUSCLE BUILDERS

PLANT MUSCLE BUILDERS
Soy : edamame, tofu, soymilk
Nuts : almonds, peanuts, peanut butter (+++ fat)
Seeds : pumpkin, squash seeds (++ fat)
Legumes : black beans, white beans, kidney beans, pinto beans, lentils

ANIMAL MUSCLE BUILDERS
Eggs (+ fat)
Canned tuna, in water
Chicken or turkey
White fish
Omega-3 rich fish (+ fat) : trout, salmon, sardines, mackerel,
Seafood : nordic shrimp, scallops, mussels,
Oysters lean
Beef (+ fat)
Lean lamb (+ fat)
Dairy : milk, yogurt, low fat cheese (+ fat)

POWDERED MUSCLE BUILDERS
Milk derived : whey protein isolate
Plant derived : soy, hemp, rice, pumpkin

FOODS THAT ENHANCE FLAVORS

Mint
Cinnamon
Vanilla
Basil
Lemons & limes
Cocoa
Mustard
Broth (chicken, vegetable, Beef, ...)

Go to: www.EatThisForPerformance.com/Hockey

People tend to eat the same main meals over and over. There is no single magic food that will give you the nutrition edge, so you need to eat a variety of foods. By increasing the variety of foods that you eat, you will increase the overall quality of your diet. Food guides can definitely help to give you an idea of what to eat. You need to be more careful about what you eat than people who are not athletes. What you put in your body has a direct effect on how you perform on the ice. Hockey players who say that they don't pay attention to what they eat and still manage to perform will never know how much better they could play if they did eat well. They don't have the nutrition edge!

SPORTS RD SAYS:

Even if you are old enough to drink alcohol, keep in mind that alcohol does nothing to help performance. Alcohol is high in calories and can slow down your recovery process after a practice or game, so it is more likely to hurt your performance. It is ideal to avoid drinking alcohol during a competitive hockey season to perform at your best.

SECTION 2: Nutrition Know-How

12. HOW DO I KNOW IF A FOOD IS GOOD FOR ME?

Quick Answer

You need to become a smart label reader in order to be a good judge of your food. The label will tell you if your food is full of good, unprocessed ingredients: fruits, vegetables, whole grains, meats, fish, dairy, or nuts and seeds. The more unprocessed your food is, the better it is. A food that is good to eat at one moment may not be good to eat at another moment because timing of eating foods is important in hockey as well.

PROCESSED FOOD

Nutrition Facts

Serving Size 10 crackers (30g)
Servings Per Carton about 14

Amount Per Serving	
Calories 140	Calories from Fat 35
	% Daily Value*
Total Fat 4g	**6%**
Saturated Fat 1.5g	**8%**
Trans Fat 0g	
Polyunsaturated Fat 0.5g	
Monounsaturated Fat 1g	
Cholesterol 0mg	**0%**
Sodium 270mg	**11%**
Total Carbohydrate 21g	**7%**
Dietary Fiber less than 1g	**3%**
Sugars 3g	
Protein 2g	
Iron 6%	

Not a significant source of vitamin A, vitamin C and calcium.

* Percent Daily Values are based on a 2,000 calorie diet. Your daily values may be higher or lower depending on your calorie needs.

	Calories:	2,000	2,500
Total Fat	Less than	65g	80g
Sat Fat	Less than	20g	25g
Cholesterol	Less than	300mg	300mg
Sodium	Less than	2,400mg	2,400mg
Total Carbohydrate		300g	375g
Dietary Fiber		25g	30g

Calories per gram:
Fat 9 • Carbohydrate 4 • Protein 4

INGREDIENTS: ENRICHED WHEAT FLOUR** (WHEAT FLOUR, NIACIN, REDUCED IRON, THIAMIN MONONITRATE, RIBOFLAVIN AND FOLIC ACID), VEGETABLE OIL* (CONTAINS ONE OR MORE OF THE FOLLOWING OILS: INTERESTERIFIED SOYBEAN, CANOLA, PALM) WITH CITRIC ACID AND TBHQ ADDED TO PRESERVE FRESHNESS, SUGAR, HIGH FRUCTOSE CORN SYRUP, CONTAINS TWO PERCENT OR LESS OF: SALT, AMMONIUM BICARBONATE, SODIUM BICARBONATE, MONOCALCIUM PHOSPHATE, SOY LECITHIN* (AN EMULSIFIER), ARTIFICIAL FLAVOR AND SODIUM SULFITE.

CONTAINS: SOY*, WHEAT**

A general rule to follow is to eat unprocessed food at most meals. Unprocessed foods are foods that go through very few steps to get from the farm to your mouth. If your foods need to be squeezed, baked, boiled, pureed, dried, frozen, or changed from the original form, you often lose some of the nutrient value.

Unprocessed foods can be identified easily because most of them are very fresh and need to be eaten soon after they are bought. These are: fruit, vegetables, meat, fish, eggs, milk, and whole grains such as oats and brown rice. But what about packaged foods? How can you tell if one is better for you than another? The only way to tell if a food is good is to learn to be a good label reader.

UNPROCESSED FOOD

The steps to becoming a good label reader:

- Read the ingredient list. A product is likely going to be better for you if the first ingredients are unprocessed foods like whole wheat, oats, brown rice, fruit, milk, or vegetables.

- Read the entire ingredient list. A product might start off with a good ingredient and end with an ingredient you should be careful not to overeat. Sugar and salt are two ingredients to watch out for.
- Compare two similar products by looking at the percentages (%) on the nutrition labels of the two products. Hold them up side by side and check that you are comparing foods with the same portion size. Hockey players would do best to check total fat %, sodium %, and fibre %.

Here are some rules to help guide you when you look at the % daily values of nutrients. Keep in mind the nutrition facts tables and the % daily values are not tailored to athletes' specific needs:

Nutrients	Which product to choose?	Example of choosing the right product:
% Fat	• Choose the product with less fat the closer you get to the time to play hockey.	• You play hockey in 1 hour. Sports bar A says it has 20% fat, and sports bar B says it has 8% fat. Choose sports bar B.
% Sodium	• Choose the product with less sodium at most meals and snacks. • Choose the product with about 20% sodium after a sweaty practice or game.	• Soup A says it has 30% sodium in 1 cup of soup, and Soup B says is has 18% sodium in 1 cup of soup. Choose soup B at most meals and snacks and after a sweaty practice or game.
% Fibre	• Choose the product with more fibre at most meals and snacks. • Choose the product with less fibre the closer you get to the time to play hockey.	• Granola bar A says is has 35% fibre, and granola bar B says is has 4% fibre. Choose granola bar A unless you are going to play hockey soon, then choose granola bar B.

SPORTS RD SAYS: ***A food product or a supplement labeled "natural" is not unprocessed. The word natural on a label does not mean anything and certainly does not mean it is better.***

A food can't really be described as "good" or "bad" for an athlete. It isn't that simple. The reality is that a food may be good to eat close to a hockey game or practice and the same food may be bad to eat at another moment and vice versa. For example, whole wheat or multigrain bread has a much higher nutrient value than white bread, but if there is not a lot of time before you hit the ice, white bread is a better choice than whole wheat bread because it has less fibre and is digested much faster.

If you are trying to eat less sugar and salt during the day you should learn their nicknames. Sugar = Agave, Corn syrup, Cane Juice, Dextrin, Dextrose, Fructose, Fruit juice concentrate, Glucose, Honey, Maltose, Maple syrup, Molasses, Rice Syrup, Sucrose. Salt = Sodium, Any ingredient with sodium in the name like monosodium glutamate (MSG), Baking soda, Baking powder.

INFO

13. WHY SHOULD I EAT BREAKFAST?

Quick Answer

Breakfast should be used to re-charge your energy stores! You have not had anything to eat or drink since the night before, which means you will easily feel low energy. Hockey players who skip breakfast tend to perform poorly in the morning and make poor food choices later in the day.

You know what happens when you forget to plug in your cell phone at night; the battery is on low to start the day. Don't make the mistake of skipping breakfast. Skipping breakfast is like starting the day with a low cell phone battery. Your body will struggle to get to 100% energy levels because you skipped a crucial mealtime.

Eating breakfast will start an important refuelling process for your muscles. If you are not hungry enough to eat breakfast, cut out any late night snacks so that you are hungrier in the morning. If you don't have time for breakfast, get up earlier to give yourself enough time to eat breakfast.

Plan what you are going to eat and organize as much as you can the night before to save time in the morning. Put out your plate, glass, utensils, and any foods that won't spoil.

Make sure that there are foods in the house that you like to eat - and that are healthy - to encourage you to eat well in the morning. Some people like to have a homemade smoothie in the morning. You can measure your ingredients the night before.

The Hockey Player's Plate can look different at breakfast than it does at lunch and supper. The morning is a great time to eat protein rich foods (muscle builders), whole grain and nutrient-rich vegetable carbohydrates (energizers), and to eat fresh fruit (energizer superfoods).

- Muscle Builders: peanut butter, eggs, milk, soy drinks, yogourt
- Whole grain and nutrient-rich vegetables (energizers): oats, whole grain breads or baked goods (pancakes, muffins, cereals), sweet potatoes
- Fresh fruit (energizer superfoods): bananas, berries, oranges, melons… yum!

Keep your intake of the high fat and high sugar foods to a minimum. These are: cream, butter, fried eggs, bacon, sausages, fried potatoes, doughnuts, pastries, croissants, butter and margarine. Eating them will make you feel sluggish and full. Consider them as an occasional treat!

The truth is, skipping any meal is a bad idea. When you skip a meal, you get really hungry before the next meal, and that is when you start making bad food choices. You are less concerned about eating nutritious foods when you feel like you are starving. You know this is true if you have ever been guilty of eating through a cookie box due to a hunger snack attack.

SKIPPING ANY MEAL IS A BAD IDEA.

If you are able to eat three meals per day and one or two healthy snacks, you will be helping your body to be properly fuelled and ready for anything that life throws at you, even double overtime!

Ever notice that your mouth is dry when you wake up? That's because you are dehydrated - your body needs liquids!

SMOOTHIE 1: HIGH ENERGY SMOOTHIE

Number of portions: 2

Ingredients

1 banana

2 tbsp (30 mL) unsweetened cacao powder

1 pitted date, Medjool variety

1/4 cup (65 mL) quick cooking oats

2 tbsp (30 mL) almond butter

2 cups (500 mL) water

SMOOTHIE 2: POWER SMOOTHIE

Number of portions: 2

Ingredients

3 cups (750 mL) fresh spinach

1 banana

1/2 cup (125 mL) frozen unsweetened blueberries

2 tbsp (30 mL) sunflower seeds

1/4 of an avocado

1 cup (250 mL) orange juice)

1 cup (250 mL) water

Personalize your smoothie by making it as thick or as runny as you like. Add water to get the desired consistency. To boost the nutritional value of your shake add:

- wheat germ (adds iron, fibre, and B vitamins)
- ground flaxseed (adds fibre and omega-3 fats)
- chopped walnuts (adds minerals and omega-3 fats)
- skim milk powder (adds protein and carbohydrates)
- greek yogourt (adds protein and carbohydrates)

14. IS THERE A WAY TO TELL IF A DIET I'VE HEARD ABOUT WILL HELP MY PERFORMANCE?

Quick Answer

You will know if a diet is okay to try if it does not require you to stop eating foods that you know are good for you. Fad diets will come in and out of style, but a performance sports nutrition diet will not go out of style because it is a set of guidelines that is flexible enough to work for everyone!

You may have heard about a diet from a trusted friend, a TV or magazine ad, or from a book. Diets always sound good and promise great results. But unless you have a medical condition, the only "diet" you should be on is the sports performance diet in this book - which is not a diet at all, it is a set of strategies to eat for performance in hockey.

Don't blindly follow other people when it comes to something as important as what you eat. Your ability to perform well as a hockey player will be seriously compromised if you don't get enough energy from your food, especially energy from carbohydrates.

Some diet gurus may tell people that carbohydrates are evil and fattening. They say that if you restrict your dietary carbohydrate, you can teach your body to burn fat. They don't tell you that using fat for energy during a shift in a hockey game is just impossible. They say that fitness training allows your body to burn more fat (which is true), but they don't mention that you need those carbs to train efficiently.

Do yourself a favour and avoid any diet that:	WHY? because...
is low carb	Carbs are THE hockey fuel.
emphasizes one food or food group	It can be missing nutrients and boring!
eliminates or limits a group of foods	It can stunt your growth.
prescribes special pills, powders, supplements, or treatments	It's expensive. Save your money! These products can hurt your health.
doesn't encourage an active lifestyle	It can be detrimental for an athlete.
promises a fast and easy weight loss	You will likely be losing body water and muscle mass which are needed to play hockey.
promises to give you muscle rapidly	It would have to be an illegal diet!

You are growing, and you need nutrients to grow and develop normally. Any diet that restricts your intake of calories and nutrients can have very serious effects on your development.

Above all, use your good common sense. Follow the guidelines in this book. When evaluating any diet, compare it to your country's food guide. Make sure that you benefit from all of the research done by the best scientific minds.

Fad diets you might hear about and that you should avoid:

The Detox Diet says your body stores toxins, so you should do a fast (eat nothing or next-to-nothing for a period of time) or drink and eat only "detox" drinks to clean out your body. Nutrition science says this is simply not true. Toxins are poisonous substances that your body needs to eliminate. Toxins can either come from the environment around you or they come from the activities your body does such as breathing and exercise. Every moment of every day your body is eliminating toxins successfully through your urine and sweat. And, when your body needs extra help, your immune system comes to the rescue. Some detox diets will ask you to fast or drink and eat certain foods that will make you have many bowel movements in a short amount of time. Doing both of these will not only hurt your hockey performance, but ironically they have been proven to really hurt your ability to fight infections.

The Paleo Diet™ says your genes are not evolved enough to eat the modern diet, so you should eat like our caveman ancestors. In general, the diet asks you to only eat the foods that were available to our caveman ancestors such as shrub vegetables, berries, nuts, root vegetables, and meat. The paleo inventors also ask you to eliminate many known healthy foods like grains, dairy, and legumes.To add to the confusion there are different ways people are following this diet. It is true that your genes do play a role in how your body reacts to food. For example, your genes will determine if your body makes the stuff to digest lactose in dairy products. If you can't digest lactose, eliminating foods with lactose is a good idea for you. You will probably notice that many people do have the ability to digest lactose. This is because everyone has different genetic profiles (different genes). So if someone tells you that the paleo diet is the best diet for your genes you should be skeptical. It is very unlikely that they took a genetic sample from you. And, it is impossible that they had the tools to tell you if your genetic profile is right for the paleo diet. It is not a good idea for a hockey player to try out the paleo diet because it eliminates so many good sources of carbohydrates.

The Gluten-Free Diet advocates say that gluten causes fatigue, weight gain, and bloating so you should eliminate it from your diet. It is really not common, but some people have an allergy or an intolerance to gluten and cannot eat anything with gluten. Those people should work with a dietitian to eliminate gluten. There is a very accurate test for gluten allergy if a gluten allergy is suspected. Otherwise, fatigue, weight gain, and bloating are common symptoms of a poor diet! If you have unpleasant symptoms, start to work with a doctor and make sure you are not sick first. If your body can digest gluten, a gluten-free diet will not give you more of the nutrition edge, and it could even hurt your hockey performance if it is not followed correctly.

A-Z

GLUTEN - Gluten is a type of protein found in grains such as wheat, rye and barley. That means most pastas, breads, cereals and processed foods contain gluten.

DEFINITION

The Alkaline Diet says your body will become acidic if you eat acidic foods, so eat only alkaline foods. Are you wondering if it is important to consider the pH (acidity) of foods? Your body keeps the pH of your blood very stable no matter what you eat. You should be choosing foods based on their nutritive value and not on their pH. Some foods are acidic (have a pH between 0 and 7) and some foods are alkaline or basic (have a pH over 7). An "alkaline" diet can be healthy, not because of its pH, but because it includes fruits and vegetables, and avoids coffee, alcohol, and processed foods. "Acidic" foods like meats and dairy products should not be eaten in excess, but they do have nutritive value and can be an important part of a healthy diet. So, the answer is that you can make healthy choices without worrying about the pH of the food.

Ketogenic (keto) diet

The ketogenic diet (a.k.a keto) is a diet in which the daily carbohydrate intake is below 30g to 100 g depending on which keto diet is being followed. The big idea is that the energizer category of food is extremely limited. Now, you must already see a red flag because this entire book is essentially telling you energizers are necessary for your sprint sport. However, you and many well meaning people will be seduced by this diet because of its effect on weight loss. So let's clear up how the weight loss diet works. When you eliminate carbs 2 things happen, one, you drop almost ½ pound of body weight (that was your stored carbs), and two you drop about 4 pounds of water that was attached to those carbs (happily hydrating your muscle). On the scale you lost almost 5 pounds without moving a muscle - bravo, maybe? Not really, because the hard reality is that you are in ketosis. A not so magical state of being that has your body using ketone bodies as a source of energy instead of sugar. Ketosis produces some severe symptoms at first - poor concentration, low energy, and the best one, extremely bad breath. If you "survive" this and feel amazing enough to work out you are training your body to be good at an explosive sport using a poor fuel. The result is that your body is not getting the most out of your training sessions - and your body is not learning to function on the fuel that will make it function best during a game. Our advice is to train how you want to play - train with energy to play with energy. Ultimately there can be a time and a place for a low carb diet. When you are working closely with a sports dietitian that is when you get to delve into the benefits and pitfalls of diets and make a decision about which approach will be best for you. For instance, you might experiment with carbohydrate periodization in the summer months in the same way as you are likely periodizing your workouts (in other words cycling through training phases). Check out section on digging deeper into periodization in sport.

FODMAP diet

Most people who can digest anything don't know how lucky they are. The situation is rather different for millions of others (1 in 7) who suffer from irritable bowel syndrome (IBS). Research shows that a low-FODMAP diet works in 75% of cases to considerably diminish the IBS symptoms. This diet was developed by two Australian researchers from Monash University in Melbourne. Since their first publication on this subject, in 2005, scientific data on the effectiveness of this diet has accumulated, leading to more and more gastroenterologists and dietitians around the world prescribing it successfully. The FODMAP acronym stands for: Fermentable – Oligosaccharides – Disaccharides – Monosaccharides – And – Polyols. These are carbohydrates that are found in garlic, onions, cashews, watermelon, wheat, barley and rye to name a few. FODMAPs attract water in the intestine and ferment, causing symptoms (bloating, intestinal gas, diarrhoea, bloated stomach, cramps) in people who are sensitive to them, mainly those suffering from IBS. The FODMAP diet is very restrictive and used for short term relief of symptoms. Athletes on a FODMAP diet work closely with their sports dietitians to get results from all their efforts.

SPORTS RD SAYS:

Every year we see a new fad diet. Don't be fooled by them! You need to be smart and resist the temptation to believe the fake claims and pictures.

 Go to: www.EatThisForPerformance.com/Hockey

FOR ALL LINKS TO ONLINE DOCUMENTS, PROGRAMS, and UPDATES!

15. IS IT A GOOD IDEA FOR ME TO BE A VEGETARIAN?

Quick Answer

A vegetarian diet can be a performance diet, but only if you plan your meals carefully. Being a vegetarian means more than just not eating meat. A poorly planned vegetarian diet will be missing many important nutrients. If you are not ready to make the effort to plan balanced meals, a vegetarian diet is not a good idea for you.

A lacto-ovo vegetarian diet is one that eliminates meat and fish from the diet. A vegan diet is one that eliminates all food and drink that is of animal origin including meat, fish, eggs, milk, yogurt, cheese, and in some cases, honey.

The more foods that you eliminate from your diet, the more you need to pay close attention to which foods have your essential nutrients. If your diet restricts a food group (such as meats) and you don't have a replacement food that has the same essential nutrients, you are putting your body at risk. The risks can be great. Low iron intake, for example, can make your blood anaemic (low in iron), and this will cause extreme fatigue.

"OOPS, I ONLY ATE FRENCH FRIES FOR LUNCH... AGAIN!"

If this sounds like you, get help planning more balanced meals that taste great.

Vegetarian hockey players may have trouble getting enough protein, iron, zinc, calcium, vitamin D, riboflavin, vitamin B12, and omega-3 fatty acids even if they include eggs and dairy products in their diet. Include all of these foods in your diet if you are vegetarian so that you can get the nutrients you need:

- legumes (beans, peas, lentils) and tofu
- whole grain and enriched breakfast cereals
- dried fruit (raisins, apricots, etc.)
- dark green leafy vegetables, specifically seaweeds, spinach, kale, and swiss chard
- wheat germ
- nuts and seeds, specifically walnuts and ground flaxseed

When it comes to protein (muscle builders), not all protein sources are created equal. Proteins are made up of amino acids linked together. In general, proteins from animal sources are considered complete because they contain a more complete selection of amino acids. Vegetarians must combine protein from different plant sources (which all lack some key essential amino acids) to ensure that they, too, get complete protein every day. Vegetarians should pay special attention to their protein sources. Extra protein in your foods isn't stored as protein, so it is essential for you to get a daily dose.

VEGETARIAN HOCKEY PLAYER'S PLATE

16. SHOULD I TAKE A SPORTS SUPPLEMENT?

Quick Answer

A sports supplement cannot make up for poor nutrition habits. When a hockey player has great eating and training habits, a sports supplement may help get a performance edge. However, professional guidance will be needed because the supplement industry is highly unregulated with potentially dangerous products on the market.

This book is focused on what to eat and drink to get a performance edge.

The most important thing to know about eating for performance is that whole food from unprocessed plant and animal sources is the best performance enhancer.

If you think that taking a protein or creatine supplement will make up for a bad diet, forget it. An equally skilled hockey player who eats well and avoids expensive supplements will beat you!

The Top Performance Pyramid shows you the things that help your body become a top performer. As you can see, if you take away a good base diet, you will perform worse even if you train properly and take supplements. Supplements contribute so little to enhancing your performance that they are only a small part of the pyramid.

The supplements triangle looks like it might fall right off the pyramid! This is to show you that supplements may not even work for you, even if one worked for your teammate.

You might have already tried a supplement without knowing it. Here are a few common ones:

- Multivitamins
- Vitamin D
- Sports drinks
- Sports gels
- Meal replacement shakes

A sports dietitian can guide you in the rare circumstances that you may need a supplement:

- If you are experiencing fatigue.
- If you are having trouble concentrating.
- If you get a lot of cramps.
- If you want to put on muscle mass.
- If you want to reduce your body fat.
- If you have great eating habits already and want to get that little edge.

Some people take supplements thinking that if some is good, more is better. Uh-uh. Be careful of supplements that can be stored in the body and build up to toxic (poisonous) levels, especially ones that contain vitamins A, D, E, and K, and iron. Too much iron has the same symptoms as too little iron — fatigue.

Really large doses of any nutrient can be harmful. Your body has to work very hard to get rid of extra vitamins and minerals it doesn't need, which puts a strain on your kidneys. People who take these supplements often end up with very expensive urine!

Here are supplements some hockey players are taking for performance enhancement. Get professional guidance if you would like to try one of these.

- Creatine to increase speed endurance
- Protein powders to supplement protein intake from muscle builder foods
- Gelatin to support body structure and prevent injury
- Beetroot juice to increase blood flow to muscles
- Caffeine to stimulate you and reduce your feeling of fatigue

SPORTS RD SAYS: ***Pills do not replace good eating habits, but supplement them. That is why they are called supplements, not replacements.***

17. CAN I EAT JUNK FOODS SOMETIMES?

Quick Answer

Yes, a little junk food won't hurt as long as you eat well most of the time. As an athlete who wants to perform well, you should try not to eat junk foods more than 3 times per week.

Junk foods include potato chips, candies, cake, french fries, and soft drinks. A food might be considered a junk food if it is out of nutrient balance. In other words, it is too high or too low in nutrients. Often junk foods are combinations of being too high and too low in nutrients. For example, soft drinks are too high in sugar and are missing protein, vitamins, or minerals. But, soft drinks can be part of a balanced diet if you have them on occasion and if you don't let them take the place of more nutrient-balanced foods. If you are serious about performing in hockey then you will drink water, different types of milk, and real fruit juices, not soft drinks.

As long as there are enough healthy foods in your diet, you can allow yourself to eat junk foods once in a while. If they taste good and you like them, this is all right. Use your own judgment. We suggest using the target practice philosophy that you use in shooting hockey pucks: Aim to always target eating foods from the Performance Foods List, and if you are a good hockey

Do you think that hazelnut chocolate spread is a healthy choice for breakfast? If you believe the TV ads, you might think so. In fact, it is more like a junk food than a healthy food option. Its ingredients are similar to a chocolate bar's ingredients. Read the label and judge for yourself whether or not you think it is a good way to start your day!

INFO

player, you won't be missing too often! By now you are starting to read labels - this too will help. You may not like junk foods once you know what is in them.

Which one of these drinks will support performance better?

Orange Drink Ingredients:	
Water, High Fructose, Corn Syrup and 2% or Less of Each of the Following: Concentrated Juices (Orange, Tangerine, Apple, Lime, Grapefruit). Citric Acid, Ascorbic Acid (Vitamin C), Beta-Carotene, Thiamin Hydrochloride (Vitamin B1), Natural Flavors, Food Starch-Modified, Canola Oil, Cellulose Gum, Xanthan Gum, Sodium Hexametaphosphate, Sodium Benzoate to Protect Flavor, Yellow #5, Yellow #6	
 Orange Juice Ingredients:	
100% pure squeezed orange juice	

Finally, don't fall for the tricks that advertisers play. They try to make you think that if you drink or eat certain things, you will have lots of energy, be healthy, and be popular. These companies are counting on people not reading or understanding the labels on their products.

YOU MAY NOT LIKE JUNK FOODS ONCE YOU KNOW WHAT IS IN THEM.

You control what you put in your body. Be smart and know what is in the foods that you eat by becoming a good label detective.

SECTION 3: Your Body

18. WHY DO I GET TIRED DURING SOME GAMES AND NOT DURING OTHERS?

Quick Answer

It could be from a lack of sleep, an overactive social life, a demanding school schedule, too much hockey, and of course, poor nutrition. It is important to find a healthy balance between work, rest, and play. Too much of any of these will result in poor performance as surely as poor nutrition does.

It is normal to get tired while playing hockey. Hockey places a high demand on the body. If you don't break out in a sweat while playing hockey, you are probably not working hard enough! Still, you sometimes have more energy than at other times.

Often, the answer lies in what you ate or drank before a game. If you didn't eat well or drink enough fluid before the game, your body may not have the stored energy it needs to play a great game. You also need to consider that foods take 1 to 3 days to move all the way from one end of your digestive system (your mouth) to the other end. If you eat poorly the day before your game or practice, you will miss the nutrition edge we keep talking about.

Remember that your muscles have batteries that are filled with

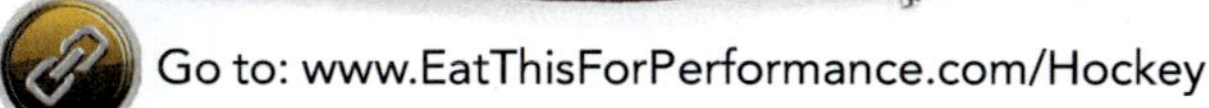
Go to: www.EatThisForPerformance.com/Hockey

carbohydrate (energizers). If your muscles run out of carbohydrate, they will get tired, you will have trouble focussing and your performance will suffer. You won't have the same pep on the ice as you did at the beginning of the game.

Why do you get tired if your muscles run out of carbohydrate stores? This is because your muscles will start to use more of their fat stores. But since muscles can't use fat very well as a fuel during a sprint, they will also use protein (muscle tissue) for energy. This means that the muscles themselves start to break down. Fat and protein are not the best sources of energy for your muscles because they take time to turn into energy. You would need to skate at a slow steady pace for fat to be a good fuel for hockey. Not ideal for a game, is it? You would be beaten to the puck every time if you skated slowly!

You can increase the amount of carbohydrate that is stored in your muscles with both training and a diet that includes quality energizers (starches, fruit, dairy and whole grains). By doing this, you will notice that you will be at your best for the whole game, not just the first period. In the third period, you will have the nutrition edge and be able to skate circles around those players who don't pay attention to what they eat!

There are other things that you need to look at if you are tired during a game. Did you sleep well the night before? Did you have a particularly difficult week at school? Are you preoccupied with other things that are going on in your life? You may not be working hard enough at practices so that your body isn't used to working hard at game time. You may have had too many physical activities in a short period of time and you are just plain tired.

If you are training well, sleeping well, and following the good sports nutrition practices in this book and you still feel tired while you are playing hockey, something else could be causing your fatigue. This would be a good time to consult a doctor to get a medical opinion.

19. HOW MUCH SHOULD I WEIGH?

Quick Answer

The world's top health professionals agree that there is no ideal body weight for a teenager. Height is the measurement that you should be concerned with. If you are fit, and you avoid habits that stunt your growth, you should grow to your full potential. Weight is not a good measure of fitness or health!

In your teenage years, you should be focused on growing as tall as your genetics will allow. A taller person with the same skills as a shorter person will often make a better hockey player. This is why stunting your growth would be the worst thing that you could do as a hockey player!

Doctors and sports dietitians use tables and percentile charts to find out whether or not you are growing to your potential. Your potential is generally determined before you are born. Look at your parents and grandparents. How tall are they? You will likely be at least as tall as one of them because you have their genes.

For the most part, your growth rate will follow predictable patterns. But do not be alarmed if your pattern turns out to be unique. As long as you stay away from growth-stunting habits you will grow soon!

There is far too much emphasis on body weight in our society. Keep in mind that genetics play a role in determining what your body will look like. Some people are naturally skinny, some are not. Some are chubby when they are young, and lose this fat when they are older. Some do not. Some start skinny and stay that way, and some do not.

It is true that being overweight is not healthy and will make playing hockey more difficult. On the other hand, just because somebody is skinny does not mean he or she is healthy. There are many people

who look skinny on the outside yet they are not healthy inside because they have incredibly bad habits - they eat really poorly, smoke, are inactive, drink a lot of alcohol, etc.

Everyone is different, and your emphasis should be on healthy habits rather than a number on a scale. You should be able to answer "yes" to these questions:

- Am I eating enough calories from nutritious foods?
- Am I growing taller according to my genetics?
- Am I active enough?
- Am I avoiding bad habits like smoking and drinking?

That's the way to get the nutrition edge!

Martin's Story: "My coach says that I shouldn't let my height predict if I will be a successful hockey player. He says that there are many examples of professional hockey players and hockey players that got full university scholarships that are not tall at all. What matters is my game time performance. Since I am not tall, my coach says that I have to concentrate on being faster, stronger and smarter than my opponent."

TESTIMONIAL

SPORTS RD SAYS:

The scale does not tell the whole story about what is going on inside your body. This is because the number on the scale cannot tell what part of you is bone, water, muscle, or fat.

WHAT MAKES THE WEIGHT ON THE SCALE GO UP?

- Building bones
- Gaining muscles
- Drinking water!
- Storing extra fat

Elite athletes get their body composition measured, not their weight. As a hockey player, you do not have strict body composition numbers to achieve. However, if a professional has told you to decrease your body fat percentage, then monitoring body fat percentage will help you achieve this goal. A health professional that is certified can take body composition measurements in an accurate way. Do not waste your money on cheap body fat scales because they are often inaccurate.

*International Society for the Advancement of Kinanthropometry

20. WHAT SHOULD I DO TO LOSE WEIGHT?

Quick Answer

Make sure that you are active and eat well and trust your body to do the rest. You are growing, and your body needs a lot of nutrients to grow and develop normally. Don't use the scale to measure your body composition. Avoid weird and restrictive diets like the plague!

You are still growing; it is normal and desirable that you gain weight. So, trying to lose weight while your body is growing may be fighting a losing - and pointless - battle. If you believe that you may be overweight, check with your doctor. See if you can improve your food and exercise habits. By increasing your activity, keeping portion sizes reasonable, chewing food properly, and eating slowly, you are setting your body up to get fit. This won't guarantee that you'll lose weight off the scale, but as you grow taller this will all help to slow down the rate at which you gain body fat. You will feel much better. Remember that weight gain doesn't happen in a week, and it can't be undone in a week.

Restricting your diet to lose weight is not the way to get in top shape. The more restrictive your diet is, the greater the chance is that you will miss out on important nutrients. This will result in your body not functioning as efficiently as it could. If you don't get the nutrients you need when you are young, you may never reach your full growth potential. You may not be as tall as you should be. You will not be as healthy as you could be. And you might get sick more often.

Really restricting calories will not help you lose weight over time. There is some evidence that the more you restrict your calories, the more your body will become efficient at using calories. That is, your body gets used to having very few calories around and you will need even less calories to maintain your weight. This means you will be eating less food and still not losing body fat. The best way to lose body fat is to follow a fitness program and eat nutritious foods at every meal and snack.

PHOTO: NATACHA SILBER

Don't let anyone tell you how much you should weigh. Don't let TV or magazines fool you into thinking that you have to be thin to be popular, active, or fit. Just because someone is thinner than you are, there is no guarantee he or she is healthy and happy. If you are eating well, feel great, and are active, that is what counts.

"I CAN TRICK THE SCALE! THE OTHER DAY I WEIGHED MYSELF THEN DRANK A WATER BOTTLE AND WEIGHED MY-SELF AGAIN. I HAD GAINED A POUND JUST BY DRINKING WATER??!"

SPORTS RD SAYS:

"Water weight is a big part of your body weight. Don't bother checking how much you weigh every day because what you eat and drink will change the number. Healthy weight loss is body fat loss, and it is only healthy to lose body fat if you have excess body fat. If you are really serious about losing weight find a sports dietitian to help you with this goal."

21. WHAT IF I WANT TO GET BIGGER AND STRONGER?

Quick Answer

Your body will get bigger and stronger when you have a growth spurt. The three things that you can do to make the most of your growth spurt is to eat well, get plenty of sleep, and do supervised strength and agility exercises in addition to hockey practices.

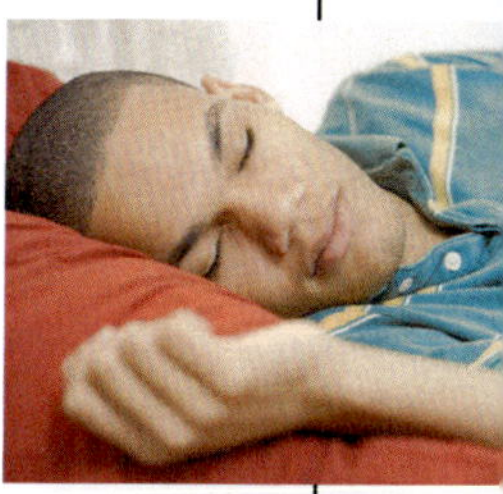

Weight and strength do matter in hockey. It is easier to be pushed off the puck when you are smaller and not as strong as your opponent. Your coach can teach you effective techniques to steal or keep the puck away from a bigger opponent. Still, you may wonder if there is anything you can do to get bigger and stronger, faster.

The important point to consider is that you are still growing. Be realistic with your expectations for growth. If your parents are both small people, it is unrealistic to expect you will grow to be 1 meter and 90 cm tall (6 ft 3 inches) and weigh 115 kg (250 pounds).

PHOTO: MARCUS NERENBERG

Your muscles will get bigger and stronger when you are in your growth spurt during puberty. Certain hormones in your body will increase and you will gain weight naturally. The timing is different for everyone, although, in general, girls start their growth spurt earlier than boys.

Boys grow fastest between the ages of 13 and 14. Boys usually grow first in height, then develop muscle mass, and only after this do they develop strength and endurance. The growth spurt also lasts longer in boys than girls, usually until the age of 20.

In general, boys do not have the potential for developing larger muscles until a year after the peak of their growth spurt. Weight lifting can make boys stronger when they are young, but it likely won't make muscles bigger until the growth spurt starts. However, keep in mind these numbers are averages only; your body may not follow this schedule.

You want to make sure that you reach your growth potential. You can do this by taking advantage of these performance-enhancing habits:

- You need to eat well. This means eating a good base diet. During a growth spurt, you may need to eat more carbohydrates and fats than you are used to. If you are having difficulty eating more, try drinking the extra energy you need in a liquid form. Homemade smoothies can be a great way to get in more carbohydrates and fat, and they are delicious!
- You need to get enough sleep every night. Most teenagers need an average of 9 hours of sleep per night. This means going to bed at 10 p.m. if you wake up at 7 a.m. Create some relaxing pre-sleep rituals, such as reading or listening to soft music.
- You need to get enough physical activity that stimulates muscle mass. Follow the training program of a qualified exercise professional who is specialized in working with hockey players. You need to eat a balanced diet with enough carbohydrates to fuel this extra muscular activity and development.

One tip that will help you recover faster and feel more energized is to eat after training. It is important to eat right after a training session since that is when your muscles are starting the recovery process.

"I THOUGHT I NEEDED TO EAT PROTEIN TO GROW MUSCLES???"

SPORTS RD SAYS: ***"The truth is eating more protein than you need is not the best way to gain more muscle. Protein makes you feel full quickly. If you fill up on high protein foods such as eggs and protein powder, you will have no appetite for eating more carbohydrates and fats - which you also need to meet the energy requirement for building muscle. Also, focussing too much on high protein sources will increase the chances that you won't have enough variety in your diet to get all the performance enhancing nutrients from the*** Performance Foods List."

22. DO I NEED A PROTEIN SUPPLEMENT TO GAIN MUSCLE MASS?

Quick Answer

Protein is easy to find in whole unprocessed foods, so protein supplements are often unnecessary. Keep away from people who pressure you into taking a supplement that may be contaminated with steroids. Seek the help of a professional sports dietitian to see if a supplement is right for you.

There are no special diets or powders that will make you bulk up. Some athletes want to take extra protein in the belief that it will build muscle. This is simply not true. Protein or amino acid powders are expensive and unnecessary for most athletes. While you need slightly more dietary protein for growth and sports, you can easily get the extra protein you need from the extra calories that you eat. When you are active, you burn more calories, so you are hungrier and eat more calories. Remember, extra dietary protein isn't stored in the body as muscle, but as fat. Taking in too much protein can also lower your appetite for the amount of carbohydrates and fat you should be eating.

1 SCOOP OF PROTEIN POWDER = 3 EGGS = 100g OF MEAT

Some athletes are encouraged by older players or coaches to use steroid drugs in order to take the shortcut to gaining weight. Athletes should run, not walk, away from people encouraging them to take steroids or other so-called "natural" products with steroid properties. "Natural" in this case does not mean harmless. Natural and artificial steroids are life-threatening.

Many athletes have paid a high price with their health for this method of adding bulk to their bodies. Report any coach who tells you that you need any drugs or supplements to the local hockey association. They will make sure that this coach will not spread this garbage around to anyone else.

Do you think steroids have a place in sports because some athletes have used them? Then you must read an important message below from Dick Pound (former President of the World Anti-Doping Agency):

"The choice is clear. Either sport should be drug-free or the flood gates opened. If the former, we need better enforcement of serious anti doping rules and educational programs for athletes, coaches, medical doctors, parents, and the public at large. If the latter, we should expect that sport will eventually be practiced only by mutants and will become increasingly extreme and violent.

No responsible parent should allow a child to enter into a vortex that will ultimately, like the gladiators of old, end in debilitating injury or death. No responsible society should permit it."

– Published in The Gazette by Stu Cowan, August 25, 2012

23. WHAT DO I DO IF I THINK SOMEONE I KNOW HAS AN EATING DISORDER?

Quick Answer

Not every teenager who is obsessed about their weight and the foods they eat will develop an eating disorder. An eating disorder is a medical diagnosis that describes several harmful behaviours. If you think someone that you know has an eating disorder, make sure that you let a parent or teacher know, or get guidance from a specialized health professional before approaching this individual.

It is a sad fact that too many people are not satisfied with how much they weigh. The diet industry is booming because people want to change how they look. Some teenagers become very obsessed about their weight and develop an eating disorder. While most teenagers will not develop eating disorders, approximately 1% will. Society is partly to blame because children and adolescents are made to believe, often through television and magazines, that people who are thin are somehow more popular and healthier. And, it is even harder to recognize a disordered eating habit in an athlete because so often athletes are encouraged to have low body fat levels. Both girls and boys can develop eating disorders, so be very careful what you say about someone's body.

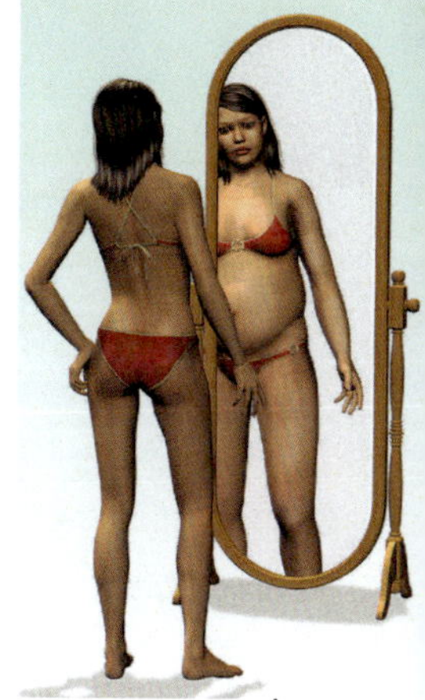

How do you know if someone has an eating disorder? People with eating disorders are very good at hiding them. Some things to watch out for in people that you think have an eating disorder are:

- They don't seem to eat enough to keep up with their active lifestyle (athletes need much more calories than non-athletes).
- Quick weight loss
- Obsessively exercising (when exercising becomes harmful not helpful)
- Poor athletic performance despite good training habits
- They take products like steroids or fat burners to change their appearance.

Athletes are not in the same category as the non-athlete when it comes to eating disorders. Often eating disorders are ignored or overlooked because athletes' routines are quite intense and their diets get more attention naturally (this book is an example of that!). Many athletes maintain a lower body weight than the average individual so using weight alone may not be a good detector of an eating disorder. However, athletes use more energy throughout the day and need to eat more to meet their energy demands. Eating disorders are easy for athletes to hide because they will often excuse their behaviour by saying that it is a training ritual. There is often a fear of discovery and denial when it comes to eating disorders.

So, what should you do if you think that someone you know has an eating disorder?

Anyone who has an eating disorder needs professional help, so before approaching somebody who you think may have an eating disorder, make a list of programs and professionals that you can refer them to. It is best that someone who is close to the individual who is an authority figure that is looked up to such as a coach, teacher or parent approach the individual. Make sure you meet with the individual in private, and definitely not in the locker room. You should be prepared with specific behaviour or issues that have made you come to these conclusions. It is best to express your concern using "I" instead of "you" to start your sentence. For example you can say "I have noticed you are training a lot lately... and I am concerned." instead of saying "You have been training a lot lately... ." Make sure to give the individual proper time to respond to your concerns and remain supportive throughout the conversation. Finally, when giving advice, avoid giving simple solutions such as "just exercise a little less." Eating disorders are a complex problem, and the wrong approach could encourage the individual to simply hide their behaviours.

ANOREXIA AND BULIMIA - Anorexia and bulimia are life-threatening eating disorders. The reasons for developing eating disorders are very complicated and not very well understood by most people. The solution is not simple and must involve professional help. People with anorexia starve themselves. People with bulimia eat a lot, but then force themselves to vomit after meals. Their bodies are just as deprived of food as anorexic people, but their teeth, mouths, jaws, esophagi and stomachs are also damaged by the frequent vomiting.

DEFINITION

"PLEASE DON'T COMMENT ON OR TEASE ME ABOUT MY WEIGHT!"

Seemingly innocent remarks can be the start of an eating disorder. Keep your comments and opinions about someone's weight to yourself. If you think that you or someone you know has an eating disorder, go to www.nedic.ca for information. Eating disorders can be fatal and are not to be taken lightly. Seek help from a medical professional specialized in working with people who have eating disorders. There may be a clinic near you with a team of specialists (doctors, nurses, dietitians, and psychologists).

WARNING

Angela's Story: "My coach told me that I would be a better hockey player if I lost weight, so I started eating less and exercising a lot more than before. I lost weight and every one told me how amazing I looked. I felt lighter on my skates. I wanted to be even better. I kept dieting and exercising. My friends told me that I had lost enough, but I still saw some fat on my body when I looked in the mirror. I wasn't playing my best hockey, but I thought I looked great. My best friend told me that she was worried about me. She said that I didn't look healthy. I didn't want to believe her. I thought that she was wrong. It took me a while to accept that she was right. I was so tired all the time. It was really hard to talk to my mom about it, but I am glad that I did. I have people helping me now. I have gained some of the weight back and I am okay with that. I am scared to think that my eating disorder could have killed me."

TESTIMONIAL

PRE-GAME NUTRITION DECISION GUIDE

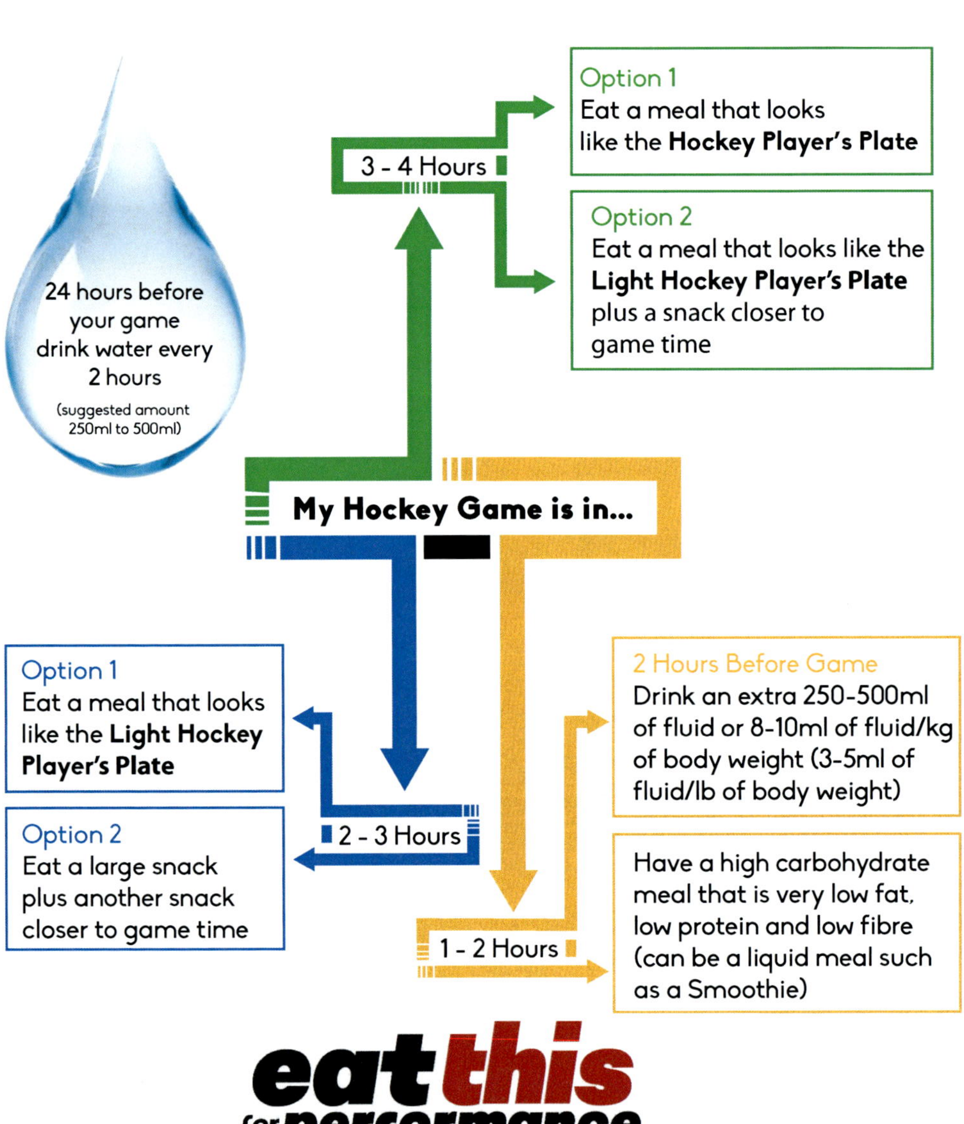

Go to: www.EatThisForPerformance.com/Hockey

SECTION 4: Before Hitting the Ice

* You should use the same guidelines for games or practices

Before Hitting the Ice

30 Minutes to 1 Hour

If Needed:
Eat or drink a quick digesting snack that is high in carbohydrates, low in fat, low in protein, and low in fibre. Check out the **Quick Energizer Snacks.**

HOME-MADE SPORT DRINK RECIPE:

200ml or 1 juice box of orange juice

+ 150ml of cold water

+ 1/8 tsp of salt

Drink 125-180ml of water.

Less Than 30 Minutes

If Needed:
Drink a liquid carbohydrate snack if a snack is needed.

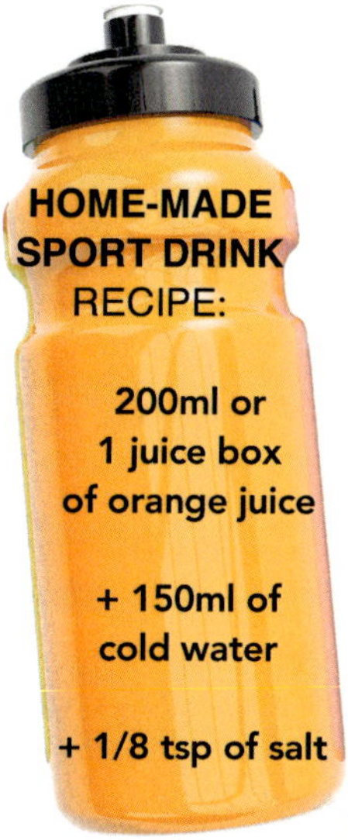

PHOTO: NATACHA SILBER

24. WHAT AND WHEN SHOULD I EAT BEFORE A GAME OR PRACTICE?

Quick Answer

Pre-game nutrition the day of your game is really important. Within 4 hours of your game, you should be filling the carbohydrate stores in your muscles and liver. You can eat many snacks or one large meal, but you will need to start eating at the right time for the type of food and amount you choose. The larger the meal/snack you eat, and the more fat, protein, and fibre the meal/snack has, the longer you will need to wait before playing a game or practicing.

What and when you eat before playing hockey will have a very strong impact on your performance. Ideally, the foods and drinks that you have swallowed have passed through your stomach before you play or practice. The stomach takes time and energy to turn what you eat into a liquid filled with teeny tiny pieces of nutrients. When food leaves your stomach the nutrients are more easily absorbed into your body and into your muscles where you need them.

If you haven't eaten enough before a game or practice the carbohydrate stores in your muscles will be too low, therefore depriving your muscles of the most important source of fuel during the game. You may even experience low blood sugar as your muscles try to get carbohydrates from wherever they can find them. Your brain is very sensitive to low blood sugar.

A STOMACH FULL OF FOOD CAN CREATE AN ENERGY WAR IN YOUR BODY.

If you eat too much food or if you eat too close to hockey time, your body won't be able to pass the food you just ate through your stomach in time. A stomach full of food can create an energy war in your body. On the one hand, your stomach needs energy to contract and blend your food into tiny bits, and on the other hand your leg muscles need energy to skate! And to make matters worse, the energy that you need for both activities is probably still stuck in the food that is sitting in your stomach. As if that was not enough, you may get heartburn too.

DON'T EAT HIGH FAT, HIGH PROTEIN, OR HIGH FIBRE FOODS RIGHT BEFORE A GAME SINCE THEY ARE SLOW TO LEAVE YOUR STOMACH.

Heartburn is when your stomach juices slosh around and sometimes come up into your throat. It can either be caused by playing on an empty stomach or by playing too soon after a big meal. Some people turn to antacids to help them with this problem. While antacids may help with your heartburn, you may get some bad side-effects like gas, bloating, and poor absorption of some important nutrients. It is better to adjust the timing and composition of the pre-game meal to avoid heartburn altogether than to take an antacid.

Antacids are a band-aid solution to poor planning!

How quickly does food leave your stomach? Here are the digestion timing rules to follow:

Foods:		Time needed for food to pass through the stomach:
Regular Meal (see Hockey Player's Plate chapter 10)	›	3 - 4 Hours
Light Meal (See Light Hockey Player's Plate chapter 10)	›	2 - 3 Hours
Liquid Meal (See Smoothie Ideas chapter 13)	›	1 - 2 Hours
Light Snack (See Snack Ideas chapter 30)	›	30 Minutes - 1 Hour

Now try applying the digestion timing rules:

Let's say you have a 3:00 p.m. game and it is now 12:00 noon. If you look at the table below, you can see that you can have a light meal. If you had wanted to eat a regular meal, you should have started eating between 10:00 and 11:00 a.m. If you have an early morning game or practice (we all love the 7 a.m. ones, don't we?), you need to eat really well the night before because you may only wake up in time to have a light snack in the morning before hockey.

Practice or Game Time:	9:00 a.m.	12:00	15:00	18:00	21:00
Regular Meal	*	8-9:00	11-12:00	14-15:00	17-18:00
Light Meal	6-7:00	9-10:00	12-13:00	15-16:00	18-19:00
Liquid Meal	7-8:00	10-11:00	13-14:00	16-17:00	19-20:00
Light Snack	8-8:30	11-11:30	14-14:30	17-17:30	20-20:30

*An extra meal should be eaten the night before if you are playing an early morning game.

It is also important to know that some foods stay longer in your stomach (they are slow to digest) because of the nutrients they contain.

Get to know the slow nutrients and the fast nutrients well:

Nutrients:	Food Examples:	SLOW or FAST nutrient?
High Fat	Nuts, Oily sauce, Fried food	VERY SLOW to leave the stomach
High Fibre	Broccoli, Beans, Bran flakes	SLOW to leave the stomach
High Protein	Meat, Dairy, Eggs	SLOW to leave the stomach
Carbohydrates	Bread, Pasta, Fruit	FAST to leave the stomach

Don't eat high fat, high protein, or high fibre foods right before a game since they are slow to leave your stomach. They will sit like rocks in your stomach and sap your energy. This makes eating poutine* right before a game one of the worst choices! Eating a large plate full of broccoli and beans right before a game is not much better!

*Poutine is a Canadian fast food combination of French fries, curd cheese, and gravy.

It is normal to get nervous before a big game. Hockey players react differently to this nervousness. Some lose their appetite and others get hungry. Some players will feel nauseous and uncomfortable if they have any food in their stomachs. Other players get the symptoms of low blood sugar very easily and need to have something in their stomachs at game time. If you know that you get nervous before a big game and your throat seems to get dry and tighten up (making eating very difficult), you have to make extra sure that you eat well in the day and hours before the game. This way, your muscles will have the fuel they need and you won't have to eat when you are nervous.

PHOTO: MARCUS NERENBERG

Never try something new before a game - like having a liquid meal when you've never had one before! You have to know what works for you. Experiment with different foods and drinks before practices. Do not start radically changing your diet on game days; you do not want to have any surprises during the game. Stick to what's familiar.

25. IS IT IMPORTANT TO DRINK MORE BEFORE A GAME?

Quick Answer

Yes, pre-game hydration is extremely important. Unless you already drink a lot of water, you should drink extra fluids (preferably water) 24 hours before playing hockey, two hours before a game or practice and again right before hitting the ice if you are showing signs of dehydration.

You should aim to drink fluids regularly in the 24 hours before a game to maximize your on-ice performance. Your body won't be building up any fluid reserves (it is too efficient at getting rid of extra fluid in urine), therefore drinking small amounts every 2 hours will help you stay well hydrated. When you are hydrated during the game, your body will sweat more efficiently and be better able to use what you drink.

Most types of fluids are good, but cool water is best. You need to find out what works for you. Diluted fruit juices and sports drinks are other acceptable choices. Coffee or other hot drinks alone are not a good choice as a pre-game beverage because you are less likely to drink to a good level of hydration when your drink is hot. Regular sweetened soft drinks are also a poor choice because they have a high concentration of sugar. If you are not a fan of plain water add a small flavour burst such as lemon, lime, or fresh mint leaves.

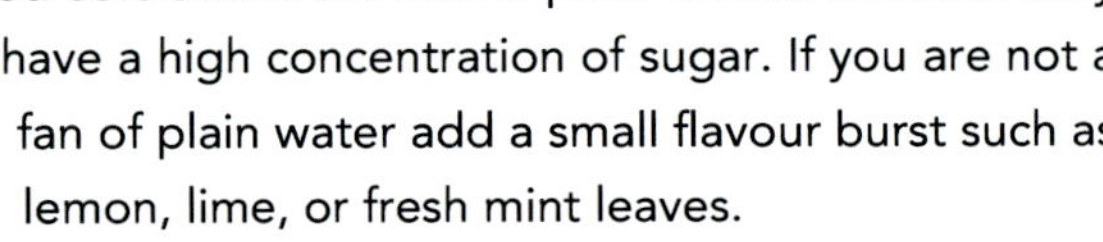

How much should you drink?

How much liquid you need depends on your body size and what you are used to drinking. What you eat will affect how much water you need to drink. If you eat or drink foods that are high in salt or fibre, your fluid needs will increase. Did you ever have a pizza meal and feel really thirsty afterwards? If yes, it was probably because pizza is really salty and your body was signaling you to drink in order to fix the fluid imbalance inside your body that the salt had caused.

Keeping your own water or juice container in the fridge is a good idea. This way, you can keep track of how much you drink.

Here are some simple guidelines to follow for pre-game hydration:

- Two hours before your game, try to have an extra cup or two (250ml-500ml) of fluid. Again, the amount depends on you. Try to have 8ml to 10ml of fluid per kilogram of body weight (3ml to 5ml per pound of body weight). So, if you weigh 50 kilograms (110 pounds), you should have 400ml to 500ml of fluid (around 2 cups).
- If you show signs of dehydration right before your game (dark urine, intense thirst, profuse sweating), drink 125 ml to 180 ml (1/2 to 3/4 cup) of fluid.

You need to adjust these guidelines to work for you. You should be using practices as trial runs for games. Follow the hydration schedule described above before a practice to find out what makes you feel good. This way, you will ensure that you are going into your game well hydrated and get the nutrition edge!

THE HYDRATION TEST

There are a couple of ways to test how much water you should be drinking in a game. This test is called a hydration test. A sports dietitian can do a hydration test on you. Then you will know exactly how much to drink to play your best!

INFO

SPORTS RD SAYS: ***Sugary drinks can give you a short burst of energy before a game, but they also may make your blood sugar dip too low during hockey if you eat too much sugar too quickly. Low blood sugar can feel like light-headedness, poor concentration, dizziness, indecisiveness, irritability, lack of motivation, poor coordination, and slower reflexes.***

SECTION 4

26. I ATE REALLY BADLY THIS WEEK. IS THERE ANYTHING THAT I CAN EAT THAT WILL HELP?

Quick Answer

Unfortunately, there are no magic foods, drinks, or supplements that will make up for eating chips, cookies, and drinking soft drinks all week. The key to improving your performance is to make good nutrition a part of everyday life. Eat well every day, because there is no food, supplement, or drink that can save you on game days.

During a game, your muscles rely mostly on your carbohydrate stores. When your carbohydrate stores have been used up, you may want to keep playing, but the physical energy will not be there. Your muscles then turn to fat for energy, which is a very slow, inefficient process. You will have to slow down your movement to give your muscles a chance to get the fuel they need.

If you want to play an amazing game, you need to make sure that your body has as much stored carbohydrates as possible. How do you make sure that your body has a lot of stored carbohydrates? You need to eat well days and hours before you hit the ice. Only eating well right before your game will be too late.

Do you eat something not recommended because you are sure it works for you? Superstitions can play a big role for many professional hockey players. It may be about how they tie their skates, put on their jerseys, or who they talk to before a game. They may feel that unless they eat a specific food, they will have a bad game. Maybe you also have a food superstition. Maybe you played an amazing game once after eating Aunt Ida's chicken pot pie. For every game after that, poor Aunt Ida had to make her chicken pot pie. If she doesn't come through one day (maybe it's Bingo Night and she doesn't feel like baking a chicken pot pie) and you play really lousy and your team loses, you blame it on her. Sounds silly, doesn't it?

Superstitions can have an effect on how you play, but it is all in your head. If you really believe that something is going to happen, you can make it happen. If you are convinced that you are going to have a really bad game because Aunt Ida is out of town, and you had to settle for spaghetti before a game, you may be nervous and lack confidence and this will affect your performance. If you have had your chicken pot pie, and you feel like you are going to play an amazing game, you will go into the game full of confidence and you will play well.

If you really feel that you have to eat or drink something specific in order to have a great game, make sure that it can be found on the Performance Foods List. In other words, if you insist on french fries before a game, we would advise against it. If it is a grapefruit, go for it! The important thing is to go into your game full of confidence, and if you have fuelled your body well by following the guidelines in this book, you will play with confidence and you will have amazing energy!

27. WILL ENERGY BARS OR SPORTS BARS GIVE ME ENERGY?

Quick Answer

If you are looking for a quick snack to satisfy your hunger, eating an energy bar or a sports bar will help to get rid of hunger pangs since they provide your body with calories. There are no special ingredients in these bars that magically give you energy. It may be a bad idea to eat one just before playing hockey since these bars are often high in fat and protein.

The term energy bar is misleading. The people who sell them would like you to think that eating them will make you feel full of energy and will help you to play sports better. According to the laws governing food labels in Canada, they are allowed to say that their bars are a source of energy because they contain at least 100 calories per serving. So, the truth is that energy in this case means calories.

We tend to love wrappers. Don't blindly trust the hype that is written on the wrapper. Read the label on these bars. Make sure that you know what you are eating. Some of these energy bars are quite high in fat and protein, and would not be digested very well just before a game or practice.

It is true that some bars have all sorts of vitamins or minerals added to them, but don't eat them to replace regular foods. This is because you can only get all of the nutrients that you need (and this includes energy, or calories) from regular foods.

There is nothing wrong with having the occasional sports bar or energy bar. They are convenient and portable (easy to throw into your hockey bag). However, eating one just before playing a game won't help you much since it won't have much of a chance to be digested during regulation time. Keep in mind that real foods are cheaper and you can get more nutrients (and less fat) from them!

28. IS IT TRUE THAT CAFFEINE CAN GIVE ME ENERGY?

Quick Answer

Caffeine can make you feel energetic, but only foods or drinks with calories (carbohydrate, protein, or fat) can give your body lasting energy. The effects of caffeine do not last long enough for you to finish your practice or hockey game with energy. Caffeine can also have some nasty side-effects like headaches, poor coordination, sleep deprivation, and dehydration.

Be careful to make a distinction between something that gives you energy (calories) and something that makes you feel energetic. Caffeine is a stimulant drug that can make you feel energetic but only for a short period. It is like plugging in your cell phone for 1 minute. For a short period you will be able to talk to someone no problem, then your phone will quickly die because you didn't really charge it!

Caffeine is found in coffee, tea, cocoa, chocolate, many soft drinks (cola drinks. Mountain Dew®, Dr. Pepper® are some examples) some energy bars, some drugs (like pain relievers and decongestants), and energy drinks.

Any drinks or sports bars that advertise energy boosts most likely contain caffeine. Caffeine can be a performance enhancer under some conditions. However, more caffeine is not better. Some athletes find that even a small amount of caffeine makes them nervous, jumpy, gives them headaches, makes it hard for them to concentrate and keeps them from sleeping well at night.

Your body gets energy (calories) from carbohydrate, protein, or fat in the foods you eat. If you eat a balanced diet with all the nutrients it needs, your body will get the energy it needs to grow, develop, and be active. You could feel energetic without any artificial help.

SPORTS RD SAYS: ***Hockey players do not need to consume large doses of caffeine to have the "energy boost" feeling. Athletes who want to use caffeine should work with a sports dietitian to develop a plan that uses the lowest effective caffeine dose possible.***

29. WILL ENERGY DRINKS REALLY GIVE ME ENERGY?

Quick Answer

Energy drinks can make you feel less tired because they contain stimulants (usually caffeine) and some of them (the ones that aren't sugar-free) are loaded with sugar. However, energy drinks do not contribute in an important way to the feeling of having lasting energy. The only things that give you lasting energy are foods and drinks that contain a balance of high quality carbohydrate and fat calories.

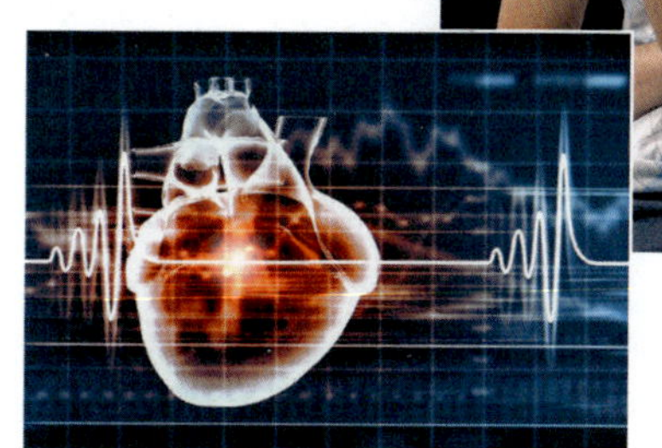

Companies that sell energy drinks are are trying to convince you their drinks will give you superpowers. These products can make you feel less tired because they contain a stimulant, usually caffeine or another caffeine-like substance. This effect doesn't last, and you will often feel even more tired once the effect wears off.

Too much caffeine can be harmful to your health. Caffeine can cause nervousness, anxiety, jitteriness, stomach issues, diarrhea, rapid heart rate, and trouble sleeping in some people. You may end up feeling like you need caffeine to function. People who are trying to cut down on the amount of caffeine they consume often experience withdrawal symptoms like headache, fatigue, irritability, and poor concentration. Does this sound like a drug that you want to put in your body before you hit the ice?

The energy drinks that are not sugar-free are loaded with sugar (up to 16 sugar packs in one can of a popular energy drink). Giving your body a high dose of sugar can give you too much energy all at once. For a moment you will feel on top of the world, but your body will crash once it starts to try to deal with the sugar overload.

Most parents wouldn't consider giving their children a cup of coffee, but many feel okay about buying them energy drinks. Energy drinks are quite expensive, so why do so many people fall into the trap set by the companies who sell them? Here's why:

- They are given names and slogans that make great promises that they can't keep.
- They are packaged to look fun and exciting. Remember, you can't judge a book by its cover.
- They add vitamins and "natural" ingredients to make them sound better than they really are.
- They are available almost everywhere, making people believe that they are popular.
- The companies who make them often sponsor athletics events because they want to fool people into thinking that there is a link between their energy drinks and the athletes who are performing.

Energy drinks are not a healthy solution to a lack of energy.

Look out for "natural" hidden sources of caffeine: yerba mate, guarana, and ilex guayusa. Remember, natural does not mean it is better! So, do not be fooled by claims that these sources of caffeine are better than any other source.

30. IT IS ALMOST GAME TIME AND I AM HUNGRY - WHAT CAN I EAT?

Quick Answer

While it is important to have properly fueled muscles during your game, it is just as important not to have food sitting undigested in your stomach while you play. From 2 hours to 5 minutes before you hit the ice, choose foods that are low in protein, fat, and fibre because these nutrients take longer to be digested.

It is always best to plan what you are going to eat in advance, especially on game days. Target eating from the Performance Foods List all the time. Life sometimes doesn't always go according to plan, though, even with the best intentions! If you are facing a situation where you are hungry and you have less than 2 hours before you hit the ice, you need to think about digestion times of foods to decide what you can eat and what you should avoid. Keep in mind that you know your body the best, and you may digest certain foods faster or slower than other people.

Foods that are high in protein, fat, and fibre are generally not recommended less than 60 minutes before game time. Your body will not have a chance to digest them before you hit the ice. Some examples are: protein bars, salads, muffins, raw whole vegetables, french fries, hamburgers, or hotdogs. A lot of the foods that are sold in arenas are not recommended to eat just before the game.

If you really only have a short time before you go on the ice, here are some snack options that might help stave off the hunger pains and leave your stomach quickly:

ENERGIZER SNACKS

- Simple milkshake (some juice and low-fat yogourt blended together.) Normally, you can add fresh fruit and skim milk powder to a milk shake to boost the nutrition content, but this isn't recommended if you don't have time to properly digest them. If you are lactose intolerant, a milkshake made with low-fat, lactose-free milk or soy milk would do the trick!
- Dried fruits (raisins, cranberries, etc.) or fruit bars. Make sure to drink water with this snack.
- Unsweetened fruit juice
- Bowl of cereal and milk
- Low fat granola bars
- White bread
- Rice cakes
- If you are really stuck and you don't have anything available to eat and you are hungry, then drinking a sports drink just before and during the game is a last resort.

Stay away from chocolate bars before hockey. They contain lots of fat and usually too much sugar. The fat in the chocolate bar may sit in your stomach like a rock and make you feel sluggish. Why would you want this before a game?

WARNING

SPORTS RD SAYS:

Why is fibre sometimes good for you and sometimes not? What's up with that? Well, on the whole, choosing foods that are high in fibre (check out the superfoods) is a great idea because fibre is an important contributor to the health of your digestive system. However, it takes time for fibre to move its way down your digestive system, so you don't want to have any high fibre foods just before getting on the ice. Whole wheat bread is better than white bread and a fresh fruit is better than fruit juice most of the time, unless you are just about to play hockey.

GAME TIME NUTRITION GUIDE

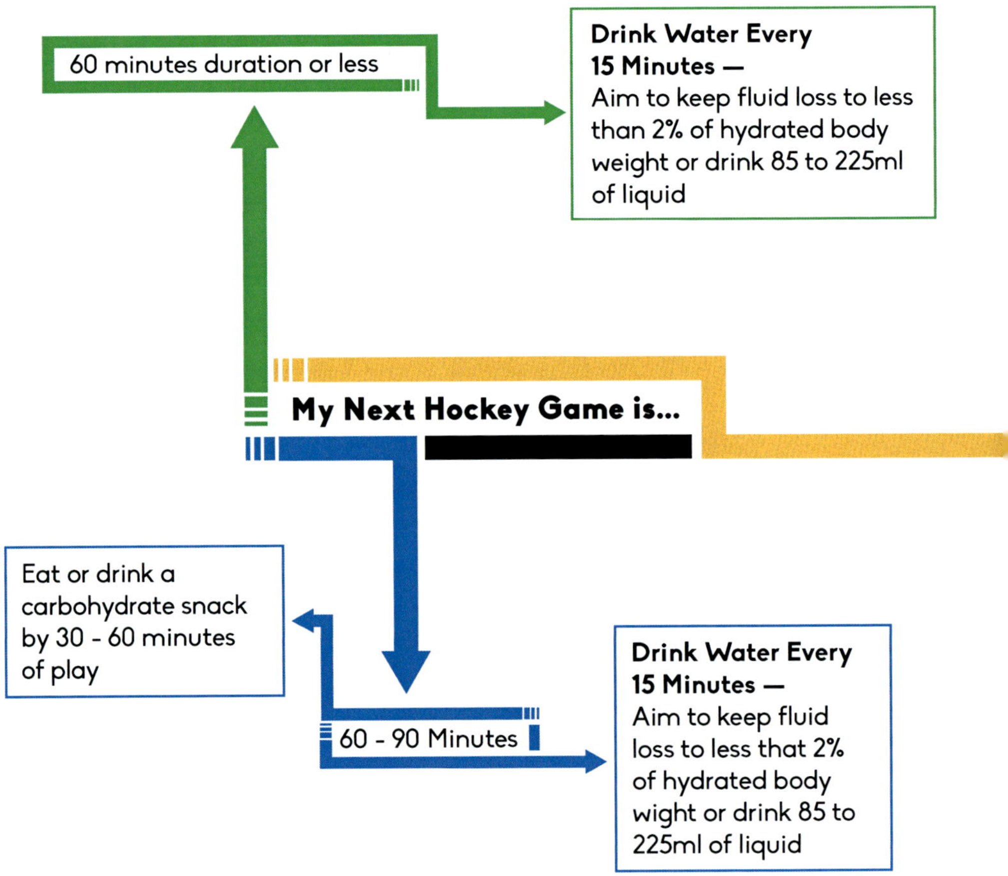

My Next Hockey Game is...

60 minutes duration or less

Drink Water Every 15 Minutes —
Aim to keep fluid loss to less than 2% of hydrated body weight or drink 85 to 225ml of liquid

60 - 90 Minutes

Eat or drink a carbohydrate snack by 30 - 60 minutes of play

Drink Water Every 15 Minutes —
Aim to keep fluid loss to less that 2% of hydrated body wight or drink 85 to 225ml of liquid

* You should use the same guidelines for games or practices

More Than 90 Minutes

Eat or drink a carbohydrate snack every hour of play starting 30 minutes into the game

Drink Water Every 15 Minutes — Aim to keep fluid loss to less than 2% of hydrated body weight or drink 85 to 225 ml of liquid.

PHOTO: NATACHA SILBER

31. WHAT SHOULD I EAT DURING A GAME OR PRACTICE?

Quick Answer

You don't need to eat during a game if you have eaten properly beforehand and you are playing for less than an hour. If you still think you need a sports food or drink (what we like to call in-play energizers) then try it in practice first.

If you have followed a good sports diet, your muscles will be filled with carbohydrates (energizers), ready for action. Most athletes can store enough carbohydrate for 90 minutes of hockey. It is only after playing hockey for 90 minutes (including the pre-game warm-up, on and off the ice) that you are at risk of running out of carbohydrate stores.

But don't wait 90 minutes to refuel your muscles to allow them to continue. During a game you will need to get your nutrients from

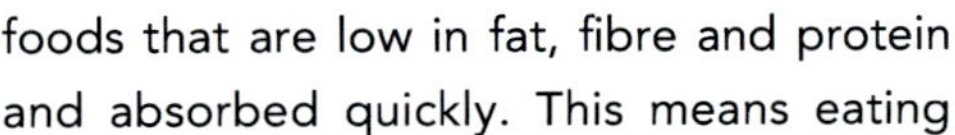

foods that are low in fat, fibre and protein and absorbed quickly. This means eating

carbohydrate rich foods. Find some foods with carbohydrates that you like and that work for you: fruit, diluted fruit juices, low fat cereal bars, rice cakes, raisins, and crackers are some examples. You may find that you always run out of steam at the end of a session that lasts 60 to 90 minutes. You can experiment with eating a light carbohydrate snack after 30 to 60 minutes into a 90-minute practice. Try a piece of fruit or a drink such as a sports drink. See if this helps boost your energy until the end of practice. If this works well for you during practice, try having either the same snack or drink between the second and third periods of a game.

PHOTO: LILYANA VYNOGRADOVA

YOU DON'T NEED TO EAT DURING A GAME IF YOU HAVE EATEN PROPERLY BEFOREHAND AND YOU ARE PLAYING FOR LESS THAN AN HOUR.

Remember, everyone is different, and there are always exceptions. Just because the general rule says that you don't need to eat if you've eaten well beforehand, your body could be the one that works differently. Many athletes do actually perform better when they eat carbohydrate foods or drinks all throughout their sport (in-play energizers). You have to find out what works for you.

Professional hockey players need to eat during games, but that does not mean you should. Their games last longer than 2 hours, and they begin to prepare for their games (and start burning their carbohydrate stores) 2 hours before the game even begins.

INFO

32. WHY SHOULD I DRINK WATER DURING A GAME OR PRACTICE AND HOW MUCH?

Quick Answer

If you want to perform at your best on the ice, you will drink water every 15 to 20 minutes, whether or not you are thirsty. How much depends on your thirst and your tolerance.

Water is essential to any diet. We need it not only to transport food and oxygen throughout the body but also to eliminate waste and regulate body temperature. We can survive a few days without food, but we will die within a few days without water. It is very important that you develop good drinking habits to play your best hockey.

Your body is composed of approximately 55 to 60 percent water. While you play hockey, you lose part of this water as sweat. You need to replace that water or you could become dehydrated (not enough fluid) and overheated. Your hockey performance can suffer as a result of even a small loss (2 per cent) in body weight from dehydration.

The consequences of severe dehydration are serious: increased body temperature, heat cramps, chills, nausea, clammy skin, rapid pulse, gastrointestinal problems, dizziness, headache, dry mouth, fatigue, heat stroke, hallucinations, swollen tongue, high body temperature, unsteady walk. Scary stuff!

IF YOU WANT A SPECIFIC AMOUNT TO DRINK, START WITH:

85 to 225 ml of liquid every 15 to 20 minutes.

Thirst may not always be a good signal. You may not always feel thirsty during and after hockey when your body would benefit from water. If you have dark coloured pee, or if you lose 2% of your body weight during hockey you should try out a new hydration plan. The habit of drinking every 15 to 20 minutes will help keep you hydrated. The amount of liquid you need depends on your body size and how much you sweat.

It can be difficult to measure how much you drink while you are playing. It helps if you do not share a water bottle so you get a good idea of how much you drink. With experience, you will come to know how much you need.

Have you ever thought that drinking water during exercise will give you cramps? This is a myth! It is the opposite... drinking water will actually help prevent muscle cramps.

Often practices are more physically demanding than games. Shifts can be quite short during a game, but during practice you are on the ice for the whole time. For long practices lasting 90 minutes or longer, your coach should allow time for you and your teammates to drink every 15 to 20 minutes. Get into the habit of drinking. It will allow you to stay motivated and to keep working hard.

Have you ever felt like you have NO appetite after hockey? This may mean that you are dehydrated. A sign of significant dehydration is loss of appetite.

INFO

SPORTS RD SAYS: *In one study by researchers at the University of Guelph in Canada, sweat rate of elite male hockey players from the OHL was evaluated to be approximately 1.5L per hour and sodium losses was approximately 2500mg per hour. You probably sweat less than these players, but these numbers will give you an idea of just how much fluid and sodium you can lose.*

33. WHAT IS THE BEST DRINK TO HAVE DURING A GAME OR PRACTICE?

Quick Answer

Cool to cold water is the best drink for games and practices that last 60 minutes or less. For really intense practices lasting longer than 90 minutes, have a Quick Energizer Snack such as a sports drink or equivalent. We call these in-play energizers because they usually contain energy you can use right away during a practice or a game.

Water is all you will need for any activity lasting less than 60 minutes. Contrary to what some people think, a cool drink will not cause cramps. The ideal drink temperature is between 15 to 20 degrees Celsius (just below room temperature, and just above most arena temperatures).

Sports drinks, in-play energizers, were designed to be used by competitive athletes to quickly replace fluid and carbohydrate losses from heavy sweating. Sports drinks are an unnecessary expense for many hockey situations. The situations when a sports drink may be beneficial are when multiple games are being played in one day or when games are longer than 60 minutes. Sports drinks deliver water, electrolytes, and carbohydrates in the form of simple sugars (sucrose, glucose, fructose, and maltodextrins) to the body quickly. There is no hard rule that says exactly when the best time is for a hockey player to drink sports drinks instead of plain water. If you usually play 90 minutes of hockey, you may

PHOTO: NATACHA SILBER

want to start drinking a sports drink after 30 minutes, even though you will not need the extra energy for 1 hour.

If you ate properly before your game, sports drinks might give you unnecessary calories that you don't need during a game. Some drinks look like sports drinks but are too concentrated and aren't tolerated as well, sometimes causing abdominal cramps, diarrhea, and dehydration. Not a pleasant situation when you are playing hockey, or any time for that matter.

Water can be unexciting, so you may find yourself drinking more often if your drink is a sport drink. If this sounds like you, a sport drink may help keep you hydrated. Make sure that it has about 15 grams of sugar or less per 250ml serving. (Read the label, smart label readers!)

Can fruit juice make a good sport drink?

Fruit juices can cause stomach cramps if consumed during a game because of their high natural sugar content. Check your orange juice label. It will probably show you that orange juice has 23 grams of sugar per 250ml serving. This is too much sugar for the amount of liquid. Some athletes like to use orange juice anyway, so they add water to dilute the sugar. By adding 150ml of water to a 200ml serving of orange juice (or other fruit juice) you will have a more tolerable concentration of sugar to water. You might want to make this mixture into a home-made sport drink!

SPORTS RD SAYS:

How much you move and how much you sweat will determine if you need a sports drink during a game. Have someone time how much of the game you spend in movement (that means skating, getting up from the ice, and moving your upper body, not sitting on the bench). There is a Playing Time Journal to help you with this task. Are you moving intensely for more than 15 minutes in a game? If not, you probably do not need a sport drink to keep you energized.

POST-GAME NUTRITION DECISION GUIDE

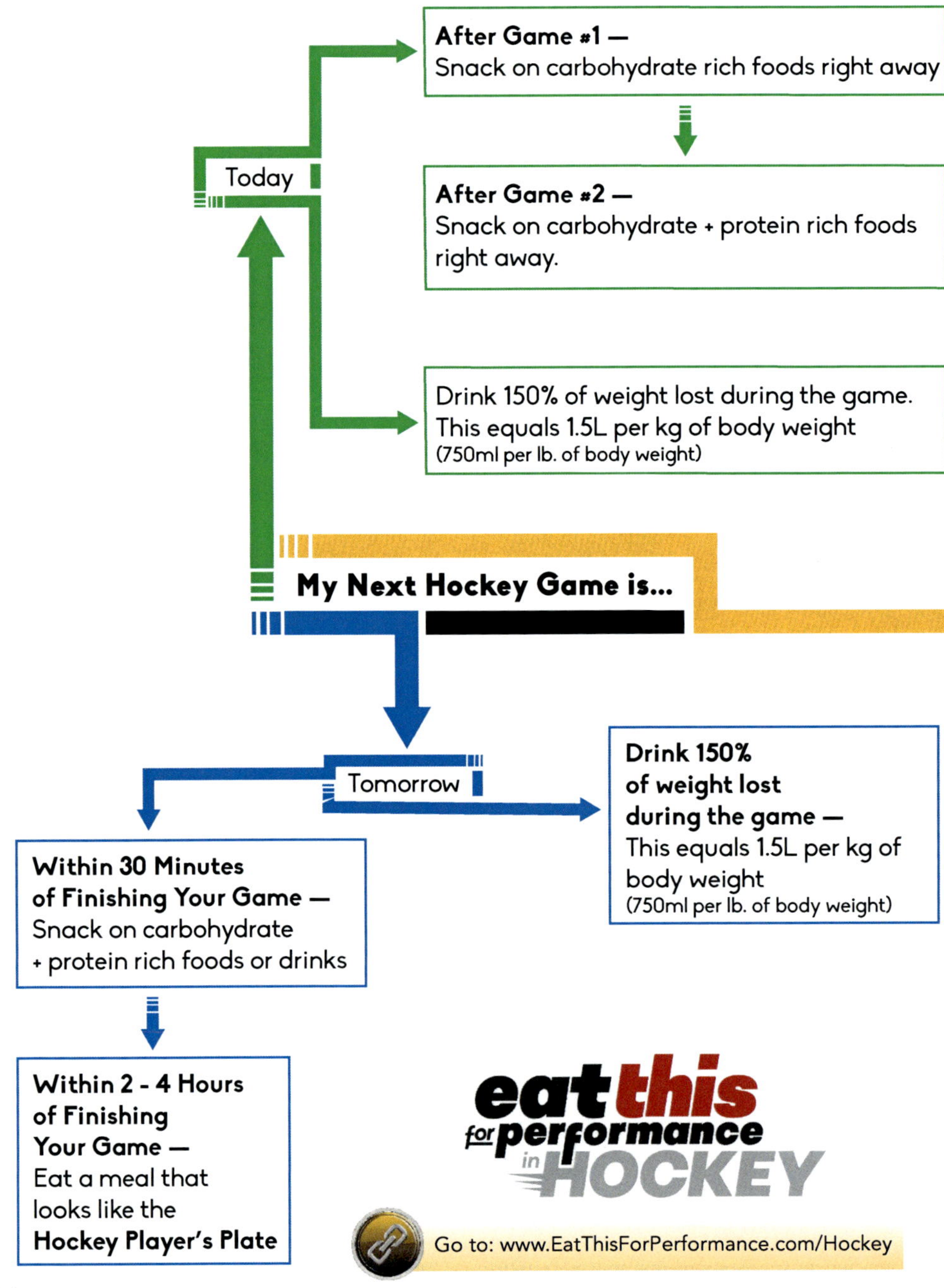

SECTION 6: After the Game

* You should use the same guidelines for games or practices

In 2 Days or More

Within 2 - 4 Hours of Finishing Your Game —
Eat a meal that looks like the **Hockey Player's Plate**.
If this is not possible, then snack on carbohydrate + protein rich foods right after the game.

Drink 150% of weight lost during the game —
This equals 1.5L per kg of body weight
(750ml per lb. of body weight)

PHOTO: NATACHA SILBER

34. WHAT SHOULD I EAT AFTER I PLAY HOCKEY?

Quick Answer

If you have a day to rest before you hit the ice again, just make sure that you eat well, following the guidelines in this book. If you are on the ice again within a day, it is important to eat carbohydrate and protein rich snacks in the locker room right after you get off the ice and a good, high carbohydrate meal within two to four hours after your game or practice see Hockey Player's Plate).

After a hockey game or practice, the carbohydrate stores in muscles need to be replenished. A good quality carbohydrate meal and 24 hours of rest are what the muscles need to refuel. If you have three or four workouts per week, don't worry about a specific recovery diet since the muscles have time to refuel.

If you have less than 24 hours between hockey events (like when you are at a hockey camp, a tournament, or have a tough regular season schedule), what you eat after exercise is especially important. You need to speed up the rate at which your muscles refuel, rehydrate, and rebuild.

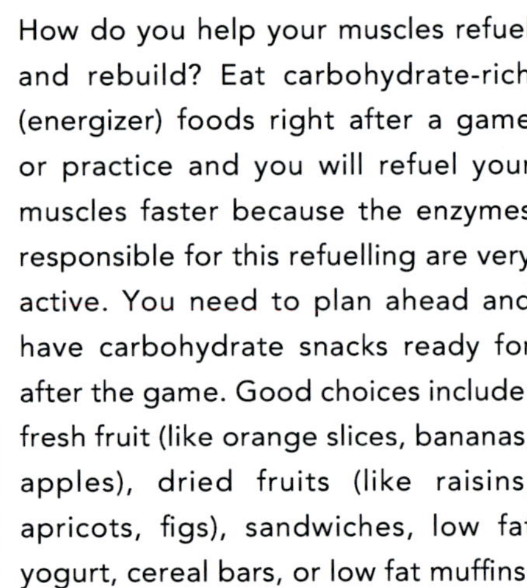

How do you help your muscles refuel and rebuild? Eat carbohydrate-rich (energizer) foods right after a game or practice and you will refuel your muscles faster because the enzymes responsible for this refuelling are very active. You need to plan ahead and have carbohydrate snacks ready for after the game. Good choices include: fresh fruit (like orange slices, bananas, apples), dried fruits (like raisins, apricots, figs), sandwiches, low fat yogurt, cereal bars, or low fat muffins.

Exercise and dehydration can dull your appetite, so you have to make sure that there are foods that you like on hand, so that you will feel like eating them. Eating a good carbohydrate-rich meal within two to four hours of the game or practice will also speed up the process of muscle refuelling.

To rebuild your muscles you will need the muscle builders: protein. You do not need to eat a huge amount of protein; a simple glass of milk and a peanut-butter sandwich will do just fine. Rehydration is not to be forgotten either! Try finding your perfect after-hockey snack that contains carbohydrates, protein, and water.

Can you believe your coaches are telling you to drink chocolate milk after a game? It's true that the perfect time to enjoy this sweet treat is within 30 minutes of a hard hockey game or practice. Lactose intolerant? Have chocolate soymilk instead!

INFO

SPORTS RD SAYS:

Follow the 3 R's after games and practices ***(see Chapter 40 for more information):***

REFUEL.

REHYDRATE.

REBUILD.

SECTION 6

35. WHAT SHOULD I DRINK AFTER I PLAY HOCKEY?

Quick Answer

Water, water, and more water. Post-game rehydration should be your top priority. For every kilogram (2.2 pounds) of water that you lose during a game, you should be drinking 1.5L (6 cups) of water. Sodium is also a great nutrient to have in your drink or in your foods after hockey. Sodium can help you rehydrate better.

Your body (including your muscles) has lost a lot of water during a game. You need to give it back what it has lost so that you can be ready for the next physical challenge. This is especially important if you are playing again within 24 hours.

Water is the fluid that you will need to drink the most. Drinks with caffeine (like coffee or cola drinks) are poor choices since caffeine is a stimulant and your goal is to relax and recover after a game, not be stimulated. Water is a great choice from a rehydration point of view, but it doesn't provide any carbohydrates, so you need to add a carbohydrate snack if you only drink water after a game.

Go to: www.EatThisForPerformance.com/Hockey

HYDRATION TEST

To re-hydrate, drink 150% of what you lost as weight.
For every pound you lose, you should drink 750ml (3 cups) of water.

(Or for every kilogram you lose, drink 1.5 liters of water.)

If you want to know exactly how much to drink after a game, weigh yourself before and after the game. This is a simple hydration test.

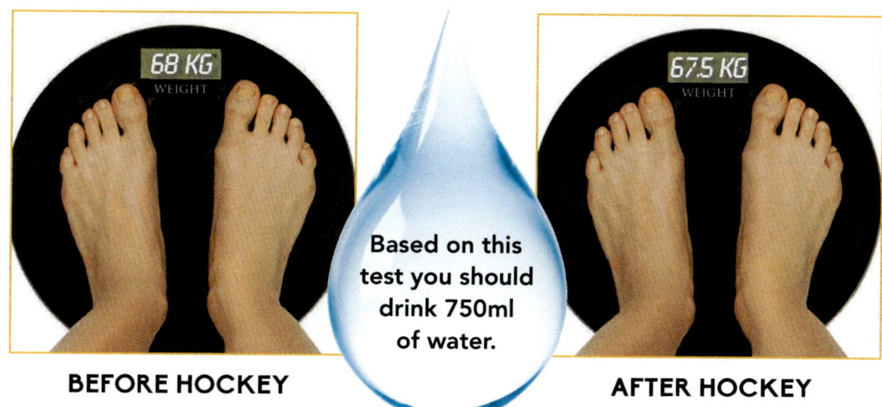

As you might know, thirst isn't a very good indicator of your level of dehydration. You may not be thirsty after a game, but your body is. If your urine is very dark, then you likely need to drink more.

Drinks or foods that are a source of sodium are also recommended. Going too low in sodium (hyponatremia) is very unlikely to happen to a hockey player. But, having sodium after a sweaty hockey game or practice can help to rehydrate your body in less time. Sodium is found in dairy products, vegetable juice, salted nuts, bread, and of course in sports drinks. Having one or two sources of sodium is plenty - there is no need to go crazy with the salt shaker!

SPORTS RD SAYS: ***Drinks with artificial sweeteners (like diet soft drinks or powders added to water) can be a poor choice for hockey players. Drinks sweetened with artificial sweeteners do not give your muscles any carbohydrates, therefore you might miss getting good energy. If you are sensitive to the effects of artificial sweeteners (some people report some mild side effects) then you would certainly be smart to avoid them! Instead try flavouring water with cold herbal tisanes like mint or berry or small amounts of lemon or lime juice.***

 Go to: www.EatThisForPerformance.com/Hockey

FOR ALL LINKS TO ONLINE DOCUMENTS, PROGRAMS, and UPDATES!

SECTION 7: Tournament Time

36. WHAT CAN I DO TO STAY ENERGETIC AND FOCUSED DURING A TOURNAMENT?

Quick Answer

Eat light, frequent meals. Drink fluids often. Stay away from high fat and high protein foods. Stay away from junk foods. Bring along as many nutritious, high-carbohydrate snacks as you can. We can't say this enough: when muscles need to refuel, carbohydrates rule!

It can be challenging for hockey players, their parents, and coaches to keep energy levels up during tournaments. For starters, it can be tempting to choose the wrong things from the menu when eating out in restaurants. You're on the move, so you need to plan carefully.

In the week before a big tournament, you need to be thinking about eating well and drinking plenty of water. Limit your physical exertion three days before your tournament to allow your muscles to build up their carbohydrate stores. Don't become a couch potato, but don't head to the ski hills for a day of mogul runs, either. Hopefully, your coach won't schedule a hard practice the day before your tournament! A light skate would be better.

Eating and drinking in the locker room right after a game is very important. Pack a healthy carbohydrate snack to bring with you on the bus or in the car. This way, you will not have the extra challenge of trying to find nutritious foods at truck stops along the way. Healthy carbohydrate snacks do not include chips, cakes, cupcakes, or soft drinks!

Pizza after a late afternoon or evening game is acceptable as long as you don't have a really early game the next day. If the food you eat is imbalanced (too high in fat or salt) you risk the after effects: heartburn, trouble sleeping, and gas. During the tournament, you should try to keep your meals light and frequent. This can be difficult when you are staying in a hotel and can only eat when you go out to a restaurant.

Try packing some simple menu items to keep with you in your room. Cereal bars, low fat healthy muffins, boiled eggs, fresh fruit, dried fruit, juice boxes, mixed dried fruit and nuts, bread or crackers with peanut butter, air-popped popcorn are some suggestions. If you or someone on your team has a refrigerator in his room, or you have access to ice and an ice box, you can also keep perishable snacks like individual yogurt or yogurt drinks, milk cartons, low-fat sliced meats for sandwiches, cheese, and carrot sticks.

For really early games, it is better to eat something in your room than to go to a restaurant for breakfast. An extra 30 to 60 minutes to an hour of sleep will go a long way toward helping your on-ice performance. A great way to start the day is with a bowl of cereal, a glass of juice, and a piece of fruit. If you don't have access to a refrigerator, adding water to skim milk powder will allow you to have milk with your cereal in your room. Skim milk powder can be bought at any grocery store. Many hotel chains include simple, nutritious breakfasts with the room rental. This can also be an excellent option, as long as you stay away from some of the popular high-fat and high-sugar options (bacon, sausages, home fries, doughnuts, danishes, croissants, syrup).

As you can see, with a little bit of planning, you can make a tournament situation work for you. With lots of rest, good foods, and liquids between games, you will be eating for performance in hockey and will be playing your best"

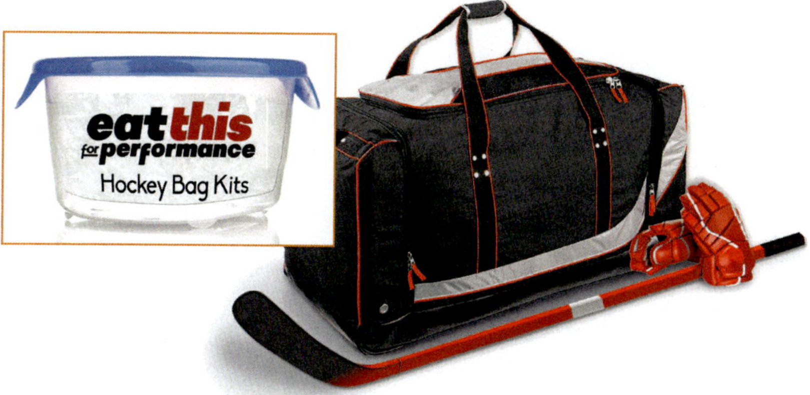

SPORTS RD SAYS:

Think that watching your salt intake is just for your parents? Think again! Most people of all ages eat above the recommended daily limit of salt in the diet. For health, everyone should aim to eat less high salt foods on a daily basis. However, if your hockey session or game lasts 90 to 120 minutes you may lose a significant amount of sodium, which is an important nutrient for performance. For these times, and in the case of someone who sweats a lot, it is recommended to have a source of sodium (salt) after hockey. So eating salty is sometimes recommended and sometimes something to avoid.

IF YOU ARE TRYING TO EAT LESS SALT AT RESTAURANTS HERE ARE SOME LOW-SALT, HIGH ENERGY FOOD CHOICES:

- Fresh vegetables prepared without butter or seasoning
- Foods that are grilled, baked, or roasted without marinades or salty rubs
- Plain grains like rice, pasta, or bread
- Fresh fruit
- Sorbet (for dessert)

If you are looking for a way to eat better on the road try bringing your meals with you. This habit will save you time, money and will likely improve your performance if you bring the right food!

37. WHAT IS CARBOHYDRATE LOADING AND IS IT A GOOD IDEA FOR ME?

Quick Answer

The modern approach to "carbohydrate loading" can help your performance during a tournament. To carbohydrate load your muscles, reduce practice intensity and increase carbohydrate and fluid intake for the three days before a tournament. This allows your muscles to build up their carbohydrate stores, thereby having more energy available when it counts.

The idea behind carbohydrate loading is to increase the amount of the storage form of carbs: glycogen. The glycogen stored in your body allows you to be better able to compete in a physically demanding event such as a tournament. Carbohydrate loading is not needed if you are playing in a single game.

In the past, carbohydrate loading meant going on a low carbohydrate diet for about 3 days together with exhaustive training, followed by a high carbohydrate diet for 1 to 2 days. This was an attempt to

increase the amount of glycogen the body was able to store. This approach is not the one that hockey players should use. Instead, increase the carbohydrate and fluids in your diet three days prior to the first hockey game in your tournament and decrease the training to allow your body to store extra glycogen. Sounds easier, doesn't it?

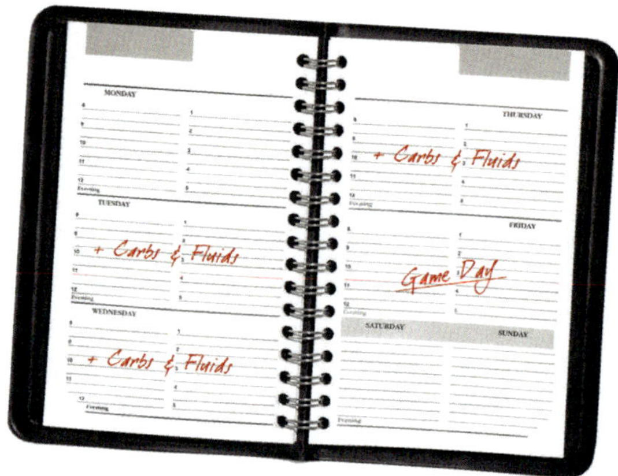

Go to: www.EatThisForPerformance.com/Hockey

This approach helps your body to get ready for a tournament in three ways:

- First, you're eating plenty of carbohydrates; the stuff glycogen is made of.
- Second, your body will store water along with the glycogen you are storing. If you get on the scale the morning of your game and you have gained a few pounds, congratulations! This is a good sign you are on your way to getting ready for the game. Don't worry about gaining weight; by the third period of the game all this extra water weight will be lost as sweat.
- Third, by reducing your training, you will be storing that energy instead of using it up.

A-Z

GLYCOGEN - Glycogen is a type of carbohydrate your body makes. When you eat enough carbohydrate-rich foods to fill all your glycogen stores, 75% will be stored in the muscles and 25% will be stored in the liver. Think of glycogen as a big web of sugar molecules stuck together. Glycogen is broken down into sugar when your body needs energy. When the liver breaks down glycogen, the sugar is released into the bloodstream so that it can go anywhere in the body. When the muscles break down glycogen, the sugar is only used locally in the muscles. You can increase the amount of glycogen in the muscles by physical training and by eating more carbohydrates (check out the energizers on the Performance Foods List).

DEFINITION

38. DO I NEED TO KNOW ABOUT QUICK AND SLOW CARBOHYDRATES DURING A TOURNAMENT?

Quick Answer

In tournament situations, or in situations where you haven't eaten properly before getting on the ice, it helps to know which carbohydrates turn into energy for your muscles quickly, and which ones give you energy over a longer period.

After you eat them, some carbohydrates are digested and turned into sugar and absorbed very quickly (quick carbohydrate), and others take a long time (slow carbohydrate). Slow carbohydrates are said to have a low "glycemic index" and raise your blood sugar slowly, and quick carbohydrates are said to have a high "glycemic index" and raise your blood sugar quickly.

The glycemic index of a food depends on how the food is prepared, how much you eat, and what you eat with the food. The presence of fibre and fat will slow down how quickly the carbohydrate is absorbed by the body, which results in a lower glycemic index. For example, a food that normally has a high glycemic index, like a bagel, will have a much lower glycemic index if it is a whole-wheat bagel with a lot of cream cheese. Whole wheat has more fibre and cream cheese has fat. If you are in a hurry to digest food, cooking your food a little longer can raise the glycemic index and speed up digestion. For example, pasta cooked for 10 to 15 minutes will digest faster than pasta cooked for 5 minutes.

GLYCEMIC INDEX - The glycemic index of a food is a measure of how quickly the glucose (a.k.a sugar) in the blood rises after eating a particular food. The higher the glycemic index of a food, the faster your blood glucose rises after you eat it. Glucose has the highest glycemic index of all the foods.

DEFINITION

Here is a cheat sheet to categorizing carbohydrates as slow or quick digesting using the glycemic index.

Things that lower the Glycemic Index of a high carb food and slow down digestion:	Things that raise the Glycemic Index of a high carb food and speed up digestion:
Eating fat at the same meal Example: Frying a food	Cooking the food longer Example: Cooking pasta longer
Eating protein at the same meal Example: Adding protein powder	Adding something acidic to the food Example: Vinegar dressing
Eating fibre at the same meal Example: Adding bran to cereal	Refining the grain Example: White bread
Eating foods raw Example: Eating raw carrot sticks	Puréeing the food or juicing the food Example: Orange juice

Are you eating more low glycemic foods or high glycemic index foods? Check out these foods to get an idea of how the glycemic index ranks foods:

Some Low Glycemic Index Foods:	Some High Glycemic Index Foods:
Apples Pears Grapefruit Low-fat fruit yogurt Skim milk Whole grain cereals Sweet potatoes Canned legumes Pasta boiled 5 minutes Chocolate milk	Pasta boiled 20 minutes Oatmeal Refined grains and cereals Potatoes Watermelon Raisins Honey Sports drinks

Eating low glycemic index foods at the meal 3 to 4 hours before playing hockey can be helpful in providing your body with energy that is slowly absorbed. Foods with a high glycemic index are best eaten in the snacks close to hockey time and during or after hockey since this is when your body could benefit from a quick energy boost.

PHOTO: PRIVATE COLLECTION, MARGOT VAN WETTUM-LACOSTE

It is possible that during a tournament or in situations when you haven't eaten properly before a game or practice, you may want to consider the glycemic index of foods. For most situations, if you have planned properly following the guidelines in this book, you won't need to worry about the glycemic index of foods.

If a food has a lower glycemic index that does not mean it is better for you!

39. HOW CAN I EAT HEALTHY FOODS IN RESTAURANTS OR SNACK BARS?

Quick Answer

Although some effort has been made in this area, don't expect to find too many nutritious choices at the arena concession stand. Restaurants that offer unprocessed food choices are the best. Plan ahead and eat well before you get to the arena. Pack a kit of high energy, high performance foods from the Performance Foods List so you never have to rely on fast food places.

When you're on the road it is not always possible to eat at the restaurant that you want. You may be unfamiliar with the restaurants in a tournament city or you might not be the one deciding where the team is going to eat. Ideally, someone from the team would have planned ahead where to eat, somewhere close to the hotel or arena (depending on the schedule), keeping in mind that restaurants that offer unprocessed foods from grain products, to meats, to vegetables and fruit are the best choices. Some places have excellent salad bars offering fresh fruits and vegetables, as well as mixed bean salads, tuna, and tofu. There are even restaurants that offer "heart healthy" menu choices, which have less fat and salt than the other choices.

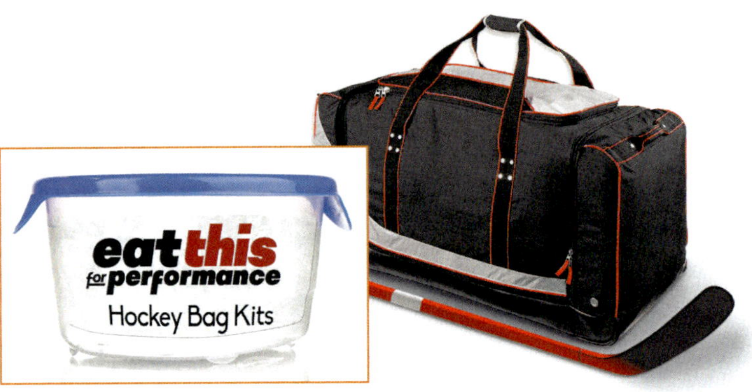

If you do not know a restaurant with these choices, another option is to buy meals or snacks at a grocery store. If you are really lucky, your team can stay at a hotel with a kitchenette, making it easier (with a bit of planning) to have easy and nutritious meals and snacks on hand.

You have to try to make the best choices based on what's available, keeping in mind eating for performance. A hamburger isn't too bad, as long as you eat it with lettuce and tomato slices - skip the full fat cheese, special sauces, and bacon and switch a white bun for a whole grain bun if you can. French fries are never a good idea, unless they are baked and indicated as a low fat, low salt option. Otherwise they are no better than potato chips. If they are a part of the meal, eat a small portion or share a portion with a teammate.

Pizza can be nutritious if you avoid putting fatty meats like pepperoni, sausage, or ham on the pizza or eating too much cheese. Make sure that your body has enough time to digest it.

Do not come to the arena hungry and expect the snack bar or concession stand to provide you with a nutritious snack or meal before a game or practice. If you come to the arena straight from school, make sure you pack extra food in your lunch kit in order to have a substantial snack or light meal before ice time. Or have someone bring you something nutritious to eat. You will see how much better you will play when you have a cereal bar and a fruit rather than fries and a soda!

40. IS THERE A WAY I CAN EAT TO RECOVER FASTER?

Quick Answer

Follow the three R's of recovery nutrition: Refuel, Rehydrate, and Rebuild. Refuel your energy stores with carbohydrates, Rehydrate your muscles with liquids, and Rebuild torn or injured tissues with protein. The sooner you follow the three R's after your game, the faster you will recover.

Hockey games can demand a different recovery nutrition plan depending on how much playing time you get and how hard you worked during the game. The greater your effort during games and the more games you play in one day, the more you should take advantage of the 3 R's of recovery:

1. REFUEL – Replenish your energy stores with carbohydrates (energizers).
2. REHYDRATE – Replenish your muscles with liquids.
3. REBUILD – Repair damaged tissue with protein (muscle builders).

REFUEL

Who doesn't like a celebratory meal after a big game? Just be sure your meal includes good sources of carbohydrates. A big steak dinner with a side of french fries may seem like a great celebration idea, but it is not the ideal recovery meal for a serious athlete because it does not have enough carbohydrates. Another important aspect of the recovery nutrition plan is the timing of the meal or snack following your game. To recover your energy stores faster, eat within 30 minutes of your game and continue to eat carbohydrate foods every hour for the next three hours. If your game ends too late to eat for the next three hours, then continue the same plan first thing in the morning when you wake up.

EXAMPLES OF A GOOD REFUELING STRATEGIES*

7 p.m. GAME FINISHES	**7:30 p.m. SNACK** (granola bar and yogourt)	**8:15 p.m. SUPPER** (mac & cheese)	**9:00 p.m. DESSERT** (apple crisp)	**10:00 p.m. BEDTIME SNACK** (banana)
9 p.m. GAME FINISHES	**9:15 p.m. SNACK** (smoothie)	**10:00 p.m. BEDTIME SNACK** (juice)	**7:30 a.m. BREAKFAST 1** (waffles and syrup)	**8:30 a.m. BREAKFAST 2** (cereal and fruit)

*The amount of each type of food you should eat will increase with increased effort during game(s).

REHYDRATE

Rehydration should start right away after your games and continue for 4 to 6 hours. The best rehydration strategy uses your actual fluid losses as a starting point plus an additional 50% more fluid. If you lost 500 ml (2 cups), you would drink 500 ml PLUS 250 ml (2 cups PLUS 1 cup). You need to have a hydration test done to know what your actual fluid losses were. If a hydration test is not possible, a good rule of thumb is to drink until you are not thirsty anymore then drink an extra 250 ml (1 cup). By adding sodium, either in your drink or in your recovery snacks that you eat with the recovery fluids, you will pee out less of the fluid you drink and rehydrate faster.

REBUILD

When you play a hockey game, you break down your muscle protein. The more you play and the harder you play, the more you break down your muscles. This is a good thing, because if you eat well in the recovery period after your game, your body can rebuild your muscles stronger and fitter. Eating well means eating a good source of protein and a good source of carbohydrate. Foods and drinks that have both carbohydrate and protein are convenient recovery options (yogurt smoothies, peanut butter and jam sandwich, chocolate milk).

Are you injured or feeling run down? Part of your rebuilding process might be repairing an injury and preventing illness which involves your immune system. Nutrition is a key part of strengthening your immune system. Do not rely on supplements like vitamin C pills to boost your immune system. Unprocessed foods and carbohydrate rich foods are the proven immune enhancers, which is yet another great reason for you to eat balanced meals that contain carbohydrates during your recovery phase.

IMMUNE SYSTEM - This is a collection of body parts (organs, tissues, and cells) that protect you from diseases that can turn into colds, flu, and infections. When a disease enters your body it should signal an immune response that will attack the organisms and substances that cause disease. You have to eat well by following the basic sports nutrition recommendations in Section 1 and targeting to eat the foods on the Performance Foods List to have a healthy immune system. People who eat poorly tend to be sick more often.

DEFINITION

SPORTS RD SAYS:

Be careful not to overdo your recovery nutrition plan by having a big recovery snack, a big recovery meal, and tons of water. Your goal is to return your body to a balanced state and not to overload your body.

Sports drinks are formulated for use during and not after your activity. The sodium amount in sports drinks is often not enough to get the most rapid rehydration possible. So having additional sodium from other foods and drinks is recommended.

INFO

 Go to: www.EatThisForPerformance.com/Hockey

FOR ALL LINKS TO ONLINE DOCUMENTS, PROGRAMS, and UPDATES!

41. HOW SHOULD I EAT AT HOCKEY TRAINING CAMP?

Quick Answer

To get the nutrition edge at training camp, you need to plan ahead. Plan to carbohydrate load with energizers three days before camp and plan when and what types of meals and snacks you will eat during the camp. Choose foods that digest rapidly during the day and eat slower digesting foods at the end of the day (after camp) during your recovery meals and snacks.

The problem with summer camps or pre-season tryout camps is that they are usually a shock to your body. The gruelling on-ice and off ice sessions will deplete your energy stores often much more than you have been used to. If your body is not prepared for the shock, you may feel more tired and sore and perform poorly. Make sure you do the following two things to prepare for hockey camp:

First, prepare your body's energy stores for camp. Three days prior to camp eat a carbohydrate-loaded diet. This means eat more of the energizer foods such as grains, fruit, and dairy. By carbohydrate loading, you will be sure to have as much energy stored in your muscles as possible for the start of camp.

Second, prepare your meal plan for camp. Often there is not enough time to digest full meals between training sessions. You will need to choose foods that pass through the stomach quickly. You can also experiment with having a liquid lunch and many small snacks throughout the day.

If food is not provided, you have a great opportunity to individualize your meal plan and eat foods that are exactly right for you. To make a plan, start by looking at the camp schedule. When will you be off ice, when will you be on ice, and when are the times you can eat meals and snacks?

Camps may be the most physically demanding time of the whole season, especially if you are out of shape. To make it through training camp, you will want to find ways to reduce muscle soreness, you will want to eat foods that will give you a lot of energy, and you will want to eat foods that are quick to digest. In your meal plan for camp try including some of these breakfast, lunch, and snack ideas.

CAMP BREAKFAST IDEAS

1. Oatmeal made with milk, banana, brown sugar, and almonds + orange juice
2. Pancakes, maple syrup, peanut butter + greek yogourt + apple slices
3. Whole grain cereal or granola, milk + banana strawberry smoothie

CAMP SNACK IDEAS

1. Try any of the Hockey Bag Snack Kits in the Digging Deeper Section
2. Good locker room snacks: fruit sauces, granola bars, UHT (ultra heat treated) milks, sports drinks
3. Good in-between session snacks: cereal and dried fruit, 1/2-sized sandwiches, sport bars, low-fat muffins

CAMP LUNCH IDEAS

1. Sandwiches
   a) Choose a bread, a protein like meat or eggs, and a small amount of vegetables.
   b) Limit sauces, mayo, and spices as these can slow or upset digestion.
2. Pasta salads
   a) Choose a pasta, a protein like cheese or chicken, and a small amount of vegetables.
   b) Limit oils, sauces, spices and mayo as these can slow or upset digestion.
3. Liquid lunches
   a) Smoothie (see smoothie recipes)
   b) Puréed soup such as a sweet potato potage + milk

Many camps will provide lunches and snacks. If this is the case, we still recommend that you bring some snacks to supplement the camp menu for times when you find you did not get enough to eat. When choosing from a buffet line, here are some things to think about:

- Check out all your options before choosing your foods and portions so you do not end up selecting something you don't want or missing something you wanted.
- Ask questions about the food to the cooks and servers when you are unsure of what is in the food.
- Ignore the choices the other players are making! Their needs and goals are likely very different from yours. If one player eats a big dessert at lunch it does not mean you should do the same. It is cooler to look good performing on the ice in front of the coaches than it is to overeat at lunch.
- During lunch, leave the food area once you are done. Otherwise, it will be too tempting to go get seconds and overeat before the afternoon session.

At the end of the day, remember to eat and drink well to recover. You need to replenish your carbohydrate stores by eating energizers foods, and you need to rehydrate. This can easily be accomplished by drinking water every half hour and eating a balanced supper and a snack before bed.

SPORTS RD SAYS: ***Keeping hydrated is one of the keys to getting through camp feeling good. You can weigh yourself at the start of each camp day to make sure you are keeping your weight stable. Most weight loss during a short camp will be from water losses.***

ULTRA HEAT TREATED (UHT) - UHT beverages are those that have been heated at a high temperature for a short period of time. This kills off the bacteria and allows the beverages to be stored at room temperature instead of the fridge. The protein and mineral content of these beverages are not affected by the UHT treatment, but some of the vitamins can be lost. Many manufacturers add vitamins back into the final product to compensate for this loss.

DEFINITION

42. DOES THE POSITION I PLAY AFFECT MY ENERGY NEEDS?

Quick Answer

Your energy needs are based on how much you move in a game. Each position has some unique movement demands, but this is just one factor to consider. Other important factors are your style of play, the strength of the opponent, and coaches' tactics. Energy expenditure measurement in hockey players is extremely variable and nearly impossible to predict.

Are you a winger, center, defence, or goalie? Each position will demand a different amount of energy from you. Your position does not tell the whole story, but let's start there:

POSITION

In general, forwards need to skate faster than the defencemen. On the other hand, the defencemen usually get more playing time than the forwards. The two differences will probably cancel each other out and you will in general have similar energy needs.

Forwards who backcheck use more energy than those that don't, which means that the center is usually skating more than the wingers. But a winger who is great at helping the defence will skate more than a center that doesn't (although should!).

Goalies have to stay mentally sharp the whole game, but unless their team is really, really weak, they are not physically working the entire time. There are opportunities to rest when the play is in the offensive zone. What makes one game harder (needing more energy) than another game is the number of saves the goalie has to make, the amount of time the play is in the defensive zone and the ability of the other team to keep switching the side of play (forcing the goalie to keep moving). One important point for goalies to keep in mind is hydration. Your equipment is heavy and thick, which makes it easier for you to dehydrate. Remember to drink often from the water bottle on your net.

STYLE OF PLAY

How you play each position is very important to consider. Some players just work harder than others because that is how they want to play or how they must play to be competitive and earn their ice time. Some players spend more time "floating" on the ice than others who always seem to be in the heat of the action.

Smaller players often have to work harder than bigger players. They have shorter skating strides. It is harder for them to push bigger players off the puck.

Players with more efficient skating styles use less energy.

Goalies can have more demanding or less demanding styles of play too. A butterfly goalie will need more energy than a stand-up goalie.

STRENGTH OF THE OPPONENT

When you are playing against a strong opponent, you will need to work much harder. You will notice that you will have to keep your shifts much shorter than when you play against weaker teams. You will be much more tired after the really challenging games, no matter which position you play.

Everyone will need less energy when playing against a weaker team. This is especially true for defencemen and the goalie since the action is mostly in the offensive zone.

COACHES' TACTICS

Your coach will decide your time on the ice. The amount of time that you play is a big factor in how much energy you burn up during a game. The number of shifts you play and the length of your shifts are important to consider. Short shifts don't necessarily mean that you use less energy in a game, especially if you have more of them.

If the teammate that you are replacing on the ice takes a longer shift (which may or may not have been decided by the coach) then you might get a shorter shift than normal.

The coaches will have game strategies that will result in more or less work for you on the ice. Does the coach want you to be a stay-at-home defenceman? Or are you expected to help out the forwards at every opportunity? As a forward, does the coach expect you to stay ready for the attack or come back and help the defence at every opportunity?

If there are a lot of penalties in a game and your coach has identified you as a power play or penalty kill player, you will need more energy than the players who are not a special teams player.

THE PLAYING TIME JOURNAL	Date:		
Name:			
Opponent:			
Period	1st	2nd	3rd
Sprints forwards			
Gliding			
Starts			
Backwards skating			
Shots			
Falls / checks			
Goalies: Number of saves + style of save			
Goalies: Time opponent was in defensive zone			
Goalies: Defensive zone face-offs			

Fill in a Playing Time Journal to get an idea of your energy needs in a game. There is no perfect tool to measure energy expenditure in hockey players. But getting someone (a parent, a coach, a friend) to video you or take notes on how you play could help you distinguish how your energy needs vary from game to game. A game where you skated hard for 15 minutes will require a lot more energy than a game where you skated hard for 8 minutes.

Be prepared for anything that could happen in a hockey game. The best hockey players in the world have to be prepared to play every other shift even if their coach only gives them one shift in the game! If you are someone who is easily disappointed if the coach is not giving you playing time, by concentrating on having the nutrition edge for each game you will help yourself win some playing time (especially towards the end of a game when everyone else is slowing down).

Go to: www.EatThisForPerformance.com/Hockey

43. HOW CAN I STAY IN SHAPE DURING THE WINTER HOLIDAYS?

Quick Answer

To stay in shape during the winter holidays, you may need to plan around feasts, tournaments, and downtime. Train more or get outdoors and move more to keep your fitness level up. By moving around, your body will be prepared to handle the extra calories of a feast. Create a nutrition plan for holiday tournaments that includes a three-day preparation phase before and balanced recovery foods after games.

As the hockey season enters the holiday season, there are three major obstacles that you might face that will affect your level of conditioning mid-season:

1. Feasts. The holidays is a time for feasting and snacking on sweets. Why does this impact you? Because you will be eating more calories than normal in a short amount of time which creates a risk for gains in body fat.
2. Tournaments. The holidays often bring holiday tournaments where high-intensity games are played on back-to-back days. You will be burning lots of calories! Without including a pre tournament carbohydrate loading phase and including proper recovery foods/drinks, playing back-to-back games can cause you to lose conditioning.
3. Down time. There is a lot more down time, so you will most likely be less active and burn less calories than you would during school or workday. Your mind might need to relax, but your body needs to stay challenged and in training throughout the holidays or it will start de-conditioning.

So how do you get through the holidays without de-conditioning?

Increase the calories you need by maintaining your level of training during times when you don't have hockey practice, and increase the calories you eat during tournaments.

1. Consult a strength coach to get a holiday plan that involves a list of daily activities you can do (they don't have to be boring - tobogganing or hikes in the snow are great cardiovascular activities!). If you include a heavy training day the day before your big feast, your body will be better equipped to handle the extra calories from feasting.
2. Limit your snacking to 3 snacks per day. This includes cookies. If you don't eat more than 3 snacks per day normally, why would you do so during a time when you are even less active?
3. In order to prepare for a tournament, eat some energizer foods at every meal (bread, cereal, pasta, rice, fruit, dairy) starting 3 days before your tournament and every day until your tournament. If your tournament is on Saturday start eating more energizers on Wednesday. If you have a holiday feast on one of the days before your tournament it would be better to spread out eating the feast over the day rather than eat one large amount.
4. Drink fluids and replenish your carbohydrate stores during and after tournament games. When you get off the ice, either in between periods or after the game, you need to be thinking about the recovery foods you can eat or recovery drinks you can drink before anything else. Your tournament energy will last and your recovery will be much quicker if you have lots of liquids (250ml to 500ml per hour) and carbohydrates (sports drinks, juice, or fruit between periods, and dairy shakes, soymilk, granola bars, or sports bars after the game).

TO STAY IN SHAPE, PLAN FOR FEASTS, TOURNAMENTS, AND DOWNTIME DURING THE HOLIDAYS.

44. HOW CAN I PREPARE TO "PEAK DURING" THE PLAYOFFS?

Quick Answer

Practice, practice, practice! All season long, turn your nutrition goals into easy to follow habits. Once playoffs have started, your nutrition habits should be the best you can make them. Remember to plan ahead, time meals and snacks on game days, and eat well after games to recover.

What better time in the hockey season to be performing at your best than during the playoffs? It is no secret that to peak physically and mentally during the playoffs, you need to be making good use of your practices all season long. For instance, if your coach had you practice the breakout a certain way, you should now be able to execute it in your sleep! The same is true for your nutrition program. Your nutrition program should now be an easy to follow habit. But, just like learning the breakout takes time, nutrition programs take time and practice to make into a habit.

HOW TO MAKE A NUTRITION PROGRAM A HABIT:

1. Make a list of your nutrition goals.
2. Tackle one goal per month. Each big change to your eating habits will be easier to make into a habit if you stick to it for 30 days.
3. Once one goal is a habit move on to the next goal. By playoff time, all the practice of your nutrition habits will allow you to be at your peak.

Kevin's Hockey Season Nutrition Goals:			
September	October	November	December
Eat a whole grain at breakfast every day.	Pack hockey bag with recovery snacks every weekend.	Eat a healthy protein at lunch every day.	Limit holiday desserts to 1 per day.
January	February	March	April
Figure out and test the best pre-game meal.	Make a carb loading plan and try it three days before my tournament.	PLAYOFFS! All goals are now habits.	PLAYOFFS! All goals are now habits.

Once you are in playoff games, there is a lot that you can do to be ready for each game. Prepare your body ahead of time by eating really well in the days and weeks before the playoffs start. If there is ever a time to stop eating junk foods such as candies, chips, and fast food, now is the time. Just make sure you are eating energizer foods like cereals, bread, fruit, and yogurt instead.

On game day, plan when you will eat your meals and snacks so you have enough time to digest. If you have one game in the day, then simply follow the same plan you would follow during the regular season. If you have more than one game in a day, then follow the same plan you would follow during a tournament. Carbohydrate-rich foods (energizers) are going to help you win games. Do not choose the playoffs to try eating a low-carb diet!

Finally, to keep your energy levels high and to lower your risk of injury, make sure to eat a good recovery snack following a playoff game. Recovery snacks need to include a source of protein (muscle builders) and an easily digested carbohydrate. Here are a few excellent playoff recovery snacks to choose from:

- Chocolate milk
- Fruit smoothie with milk or soymilk
- Low fat muffin with peanut butter
- Granola and yogourt
- Cereal and milk
- Protein bar and fruit

SPORTS RD SAYS: ***If your playoff game goes into overtime and if you feel like your energy is running low, try having a sports drink or another sweet sports product like a gel between the periods. Do not lie down after eating! Food and drink needs to digest quickly so keep gravity on your side by staying upright and you will be more likely to absorb the energy in time and avoid heartburn or nausea.***

45. SHOULD I EAT DIFFERENTLY IN THE OFF-SEASON?

Quick Answer

Normally you should change your eating habits if your activity level changes. If you are much less active in the off-season, you will not need to eat as much. If you play a summer sport that requires you to move more and train more, then you will probably need to eat more. The habits that you should not change are eating fresh fruit, fresh vegetables, and nutritious whole grains every day — those same foods found in the Performance Foods List.

There are three possible off-season training scenarios that could require you to follow a modified nutrition plan:

Scenario 1: You practice an entirely different sport.

Scenario 2: You do off-season hockey-specific training.

Scenario 3: You stop training during the off-season and lose conditioning.

You probably have at least one of the scenarios happening in your off-season, maybe even all three?

If you practice a different sport, your nutrition program will need to adjust to the demands of that sport. We cannot give you specific guidelines for your new sport because there are so many possibilities of sports you could be doing, but here are 5 questions to ask yourself about your off-season sport:

1. Does your off-season sport have longer practices than you had in the hockey season?

YES – then eat more than you did during the hockey season at your meals and snacks before or during practice.

PHOTO: PRIVATE COLLECTION, MARGOT VAN WETTUM-LACOSTE

2. Does your off-season sport make you sprint more than hockey did?
   YES – then this is a great sport to help you with fuelling for hockey. You should try the same nutrition program you used for hockey.
3. Does your off-season sport need you to move slower than hockey did?
   YES – you can probably drink or eat during your sport much more easily, this is a good time to try a sports drink or a sports gel during a practice to get used to digesting while you move.
4. Does your off-season sport include cross-training sessions that you did not have during the hockey season such as strength training?
   YES – then make sure you are eating a good recovery snack after your cross-training sessions (especially if the sessions are very tough!)
5. Does your off-season sport have longer competitions/games/matches?
   YES – then you will need a different nutrition plan that gives you energy at the right time for your summer sport. Try not to let 90 minutes go by without having an energizer food or drink.

If you are doing an off-season hockey specific training program, your nutrition habits may still need to be adjusted. Not all hockey training programs are the same, so you need to evaluate the training program you are doing and make any necessary changes to your nutrition program. To help you figure things out, here are 3 questions to ask yourself about your training program:

1. Do you train more often in the week in the off-season?
   YES – then a recovery meal or snack is even more important to have right away after your training sessions.

2. Do you train at different times of the day now?

   YES – then you will need to re-arrange your eating schedule to match your training schedule. If you train in the morning, make sure you are giving yourself enough time to digest breakfast.

3. Are you trying to gain muscle or lose body fat?

   GAIN MUSCLE – If you are trying to gain muscle, you need to eat more calories in the form of good fats and quality carbohydrates with just a little increase to your protein intake. You should be eating every 1 to 3 hours. Training several times a week will be necessary to build muscle for sport.

   LOSE BODY FAT – If you are trying to lose body fat, you should reduce the amount of fried foods, sweets, high fat proteins, oily foods, and sugary drinks you eat and aim to eat mostly from the Performance Foods List.

The off-season is the perfect time to experiment with the types and amounts of foods you eat before exercise. If you find the winning combination before your season you are getting ahead of the competition!

If you are taking the off-season completely "off" then it goes without saying your fitness level will decrease. When you train less, your body will need less calories and you might be less hungry. If you are eating less food, try to make sure that the foods that you eat are really nutritious (like the green light foods in the Digging Deeper Section at the end of the book). Try not to have sweet drinks, lots of bread, chips, ice cream, hot dogs, and fried food - in fact, most of the foods you will find at a typical summer BBQ! To keep your hockey fitness level high over the summer, try to keep the great habits that you have. Eat mostly fresh fruit, vegetables, lean proteins, and whole grains at meals. Keep the summer BBQ foods for an occasional meal.

EAT 4 PERFORMANCE 4 LIFE

You need to give 100 percent effort every time that you step on the ice to improve as a hockey player. To do this, you must properly fuel your body (before, during, and after hitting the ice) to give your body the energy it needs to practice and play hard and to recover from all your hard work. When you come off the ice knowing that you were able to play your best, it makes your hockey experience that much more fun.

Eating well is a question of balance and making sure that good foods are an integral part of your daily habits. Eating well means not feeling the least bit guilty for occasionally eating foods that serve no purpose other than they taste good. You don't need to feel guilty if you've eaten plenty of nutritious foods the rest of the day. Once you know how to eat well, especially in a hurry, you can make it a part of your everyday life.

Whether or not you go on to become a professional hockey player, the information in this book will help you to become a healthy active adult. Having good food habits when you are young will help you to have them when you are an adult. Trust us - changing bad habits when you are an adult is much harder than when you are younger. Your parents or guardians can help by making sure that healthy foods are available, but it is up to you to eat them. If your parents, mentors, or coaches have some bad food habits, you should not see that as an excuse to have the same bad habits. If you are serious about improving yourself as a hockey player, you need to take responsibility for what you eat. Don't let peer pressure dictate what you eat or let the media tell you what is good for you.

Hockey players who don't eat properly and still play great will never know how much better they could play if they actually put some thought into what they put into their mouths. So give yourself the nutrition edge. Smile the next time that you see opponents on the other team line up for their hotdogs and fries at the concession stand before the game. Smile as you skate circles around them with your muscles bursting with energy from a nutrient-packed diet.

Go to: www.EatThisForPerformance.com/Hockey

FOR ALL LINKS TO ONLINE DOCUMENTS, PROGRAMS, and UPDATES!

DIGGING DEEPER

HOW DIGGING DEEPER HELPED ME EAT BETTER.

Simon

Just tell me what to eat! I really like the menus because I can just follow them. Sometimes there was a food that I did not have at home like frozen waffles, but I checked and found waffles in the "Stoplight Energizers." I had bread instead of waffles and had just as good a game. I also gave my mom the hockey bag kit recipes and she made them for me. They were very good and saved my life in my last tournament when there was nothing to eat at the arena snack bar!

Rachel

I have a little agenda where I write down anything important at school. So, I decided to write down everything I ate on Thursday. It wasn't easy. I kept eating things and forgetting to write it down! I chose Thursday because I had a game at 7 p.m., just like in the example. On Saturday, I sat down with my dad and looked at what I ate compared to the example. I was so surprised we found 3 things I was missing even though I thought I was eating super healthy that day. I will definitely add them so I have more energy for my next game. Watch out, competition!

‹‹‹ **DIG DEEPER** ›››

Your name:

Foods that work for me:

Foods that I should stay away from:

NOTES:

DIG DEEPER 1: STOPLIGHT ENERGIZERS

Follow the stoplight guide to choosing your daily foods. Choose green light foods more often, yellow light foods occasionally, and red light foods less than once a day.

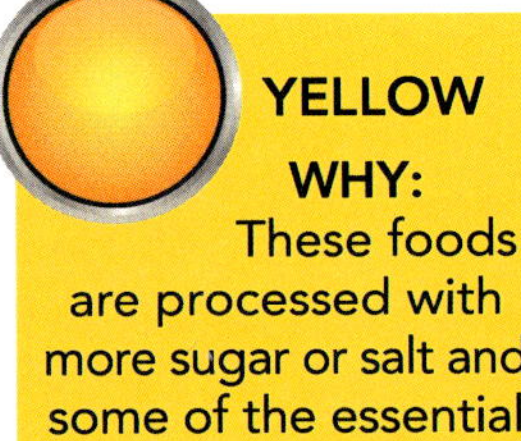

Foods with Hidden Fats:	
💧	Some fat
💧💧	Moderate amount of fat
💧💧💧	A lot of fat

30g of carbohydrate can usually be found in the portion indicated below.

GO

CEREAL:	
Less than 8 grams of sugar per 40 gram portion.	
1 cup (40g)	Whole grain flakes cereal
1 3/4 cups (40g)	Cheerios®
1/2 cup (40g)	Low fat granola
1/2 cup (50g)	Whole oats

CEREAL:
8 to 14 grams of sugar per 40 gram portion.

STOP

CEREAL:
Over 15 grams of sugar per 40 gram portion.

BREAD: GO	
2 slices (65g)	Whole grain bread
65g	Whole grain french bread
1 (65g)	Whole grain flour tortilla
2/3 (65g)	Whole grain bagel
1 (65g)	Whole grain pita bread
1 (65g)	Whole grain english muffin
1 1/2 (115g)	Whole grain pancakes, low fat
2 1/2 (90g)	Whole grain waffles, low fat

BREAD:	
2 slices (65g)	White bread
65g	French bread
1 (65g)	Flour tortilla
2/3 (65g)	Bagel
1 (65g)	Pita bread
1 (65g)	English muffin, Hot dog or Hamburger bun
1 1/2 (115g)	pancake 💧
2 1/2 (90g)	waffle 💧

BREAD: STOP
crossant, plain 💧💧💧

PASTA OR RICE: GO	
1 cup (250ml)	Bulgur
1 cup (250ml)	Wild rice
1 cup (250ml)	Whole wheat pasta
1 1/4 cups (310ml)	Soba noodles
3/4 cup (185ml)	Brown rice
3/4 cup (185ml)	Barley
3/4 cup (185ml)	Whole wheat couscous
1 cup (250ml)	Quinoa

PASTA OR RICE:	
2/3 cup (165ml)	White pasta
3/4 cup (185ml)	White rice
3/4 cup (185ml)	Couscous

PASTA OR RICE: STOP
Ramen noodles 💧

GO — SNACKS:

1.5 to 2 granola bars	Granola bar (<5g sugar per bar)
90 crackers (50g)	Whole grain crackers (<100mg sodium per 50g serving)

SNACKS: Be careful of the sugar and salt added!

Granola bar (<10g sugar per bar)
Popcorn, plain
Crackers (<100mg sodium per 50g serving)

STOP — SNACKS: Be careful of the sugar and salt added!

Granola bar (>10g sugar per bar)
Popcorn, buttered 💧💧💧
Cheese crackers fish shaped 💧
Square wheat crackers 💧
Muffin 💧💧

GO — STARCHY VEGETABLES:

2 1/4 cups (330g)	Butternut squash
1 cup (250ml)	Corn
1 1/2 cups (210g)	Sweet potatoes
1 1/2 cups (240g)	Potatoes
1 cup (250ml)	Lentils*
200ml	Chickpeas*
1 cup (250ml)	Red kidney beans*
3/4 cup (185ml)	Black turtle beans*

STARCHY VEGETABLES:

Sweetened corn
Mashed potatoes
Lentil soup*
Chickpea hummus*

STOP — STARCHY VEGETABLES:

Hash browns 💧💧
French fries 💧💧

*Also an excellent source of protein.

FRESH FRUIT: GO	
2 (230g)	Apples
2 (190g)	Oranges
2 (200g)	Pears
2 1/2 (310g)	Peaches
2 1/2 (270g)	Nectarines
9 (250g)	Apricots, fresh
26 (190g)	Cherries
1 (180g)	Mango
1 (135g)	Banana
2 (400g)	Grapefruit
36 (170g)	Grapes, red or green
4 (250g)	Clementines
4 1/2 (260g)	Plums
3 (200g)	Kiwis
1 1/2 cups (375ml) (240g)	Pineapple, diced
1 3/4 cups (435ml) (330g)	Melons
2 cups (500ml) (260g)	Raspberries
1 1/2 cups (375ml) (250g)	Blueberries
2 cups (500ml) (325g)	Blackberries
2 cups (500ml) (360g)	Strawberries
1 1/2 cups (375ml) (400g)	Fruit salad

FRUIT BLENDS: No sugar added.	
1 cup (250ml) (280g)	Applesauce

FRUIT BLENDS: Sugar added. STOP
Fruit salad
Applesauce

DRIED FRUIT: GO	
8 (50g)	Dried apple slices
15 (50g)	Dried apricots halves
5 tbsp (75ml) (40g)	Dried cranberries
4 tbsp (60ml) (40g)	Raisins
5 (40g)	Dates
6 (50g)	Prunes
6 (50g)	Figs

JUICES:	
1 cup (250ml)	Apple juice
1 cup (250ml)	Orange juice
1 1/4 cup (310ml)	Grapefruit juice
3/4 cup (185ml)	Pineapple juice
1 cup (250ml)	Cranberry juice
3/4 cup (185ml)	Grape juice
2/3 cup (165ml)	Prune juice

STOP

SWEET FOODS:	
55g	Chocolate 💧💧💧
300ml	Sugared drinks
450ml	Sports drinks
2 tbsp (30ml)	Chocolate spread 💧💧
1 cup (250ml)	Ice-cream 💧💧
8 tbsp (120ml)	Ketchup
2 tbsp (30ml)	Honey or Maple syrup
3 tbsp (40ml)	Fruit jam
2 tbsp (30ml)	Molasses
1 cup (250ml)	Sorbet
2 tbsp (30ml)	Sugar, white or brown

DIG DEEPER 2: STOPLIGHT FAT SOURCES

Follow the stoplight guide to choosing your daily foods. Choose green light foods more often, yellow light foods occasionally, and red light foods less than once a day.

GO — GREEN
WHY:
These foods are sources of unsaturated fatty acids. They are healthy fats but should still be eaten in small quantities.

YELLOW
WHY:
These foods are sources of saturated fats or they are more concentrated sources of fat and should be eaten moderately.

STOP — RED
WHY:
These foods are high in concentrated amounts of saturated fats or added sodium. Eat these foods only occasionally.

5g of fat can usually be found in the portion indicated below.

UNSATURATED FATS: (GO)	
1/6 (35g	Avocado
2 tbsp (30ml)	Hummus
UNSATURATED FATS: (YELLOW)	
1 tsp (5ml)	Cooking oils (canola, corn, sunflower, grapeseed, peanut, almond, or avocado)
1 tsp (5ml)	Cold oils (olive, flaxseed, walnut, and hemp)
1 tsp (5ml)	Margarine, non-hydrogenated
1 tbsp (15ml)	Mayonnaise, reduced fat
1 tbsp (15ml)	Salad dressing
3 tbsp (45ml)	Salad dressing, reduced fat
UNSATURATED FATS: (STOP)	
1 tsp (5ml)	Mayonnaise
8 medium (33g)	Olives green or black

SATURATED FATS:	
2 tbsp (30ml)	Cream, 15% m.f.
1 tsp (5ml)	Butter

STOP

SATURATED FATS:	
2 tbsp (30ml)	Cream, > 15% m.f.
10g (1/2 slice)	Bacon
2 tbsp (30ml)	Cream cheese, reduced fat
1 tbsp (15ml)	Cream cheese
2 tsp (10ml)	Tartar sauce

GO

*NUTS & SEEDS: No added toppings or oils.	
15ml (9g)	Peanuts
15ml (9g)	Cashews or pistachios
2 halves (6g)	Walnuts
15ml (7g)	Pecans
10ml (10g)	Pumpkin seeds
15ml (8g)	Sunflower seeds
7 whole (8g)	Almonds
15ml (7.5g)	Hazelnuts
2 whole (7g)	Brazil nuts
22ml (10g)	Flaxseed
22ml (16g)	Chia seed
15ml	Hemp seeds
2 (5g)	Macadamia nuts

*Eaten in small quantities plain nuts and seeds become a green light option!

STOP

NUTS & SEEDS: Added toppings or oils.

DIG DEEPER 3: STOPLIGHT MUSCLE BUILDERS

Follow the stoplight guide to choosing your daily foods. Choose green light foods more often, yellow light foods occasionally, and red light foods less than once a day.

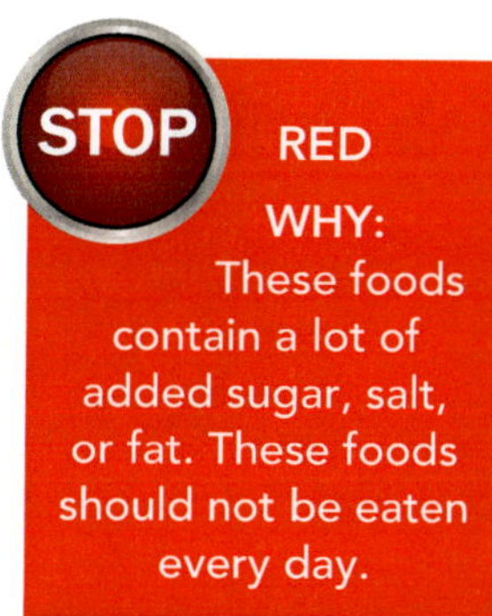

Foods with Hidden Fats:	
💧	Some fat
💧💧	Moderate amount of fat
💧💧💧	A lot of fat

16g of protein can usually be found in the portion indicated below.

MILKS & YOGOURT: Also a source of carbohydrates. (GO)	
2 cups (500 ml)	Milk, 0% & 1% 💧
100 ml	Skim milk powder
600 ml	Soy milk, plain 💧
330 ml (350g)	Yogourt, plain, 1-2% m.f. 💧

MILKS & YOGOURT: Also a source of carbohydrates.	
2 cups (500 ml)	Milk, 2% & 3%
600 ml	Soy milk, flavoured 💧
330 ml (350g)	Yogourt, flavoured, 1-2% m.f. 💧
2 cups (500ml)	Chocolate milk, 1% m.f. 💧

NUTS & SEEDS: No added toppings or oils	
1/2 cup (125ml/75g)	Peanuts💧💧💧
1/2 cup (125ml/75g)	Almonds 💧💧💧
3/4 cup (185ml/110g)	Cashews 💧💧💧
1/4 cup (60ml/60g)	Pumpkin & squash seeds 💧💧💧
2/3 cup (165ml/80g)	Sunflower seeds 💧💧💧
4 tbsp (60ml)	Peanut butter 💧💧💧
4 tbsp (60ml)	Almond butter 💧💧💧
4 tbsp (60ml/30g)	Soy nuts 💧

STOP

NUTS & SEEDS: Added toppings or oils.

GO

VEGETARIAN PROTEINS:	
60g	Cheese, 16% m.f. 52% moisture💧💧
1/2 cup (125ml/120g)	Cottage cheese, 2% m.f. 💧💧
2	Eggs, large 💧💧
4 (130g)	Egg whites from large eggs
125g	Tofu, firm or extra-firm 💧

VEGETARIAN PROTEINS:	
60g	Cheese, 33% m.f. 37% moisture💧💧💧
18g	Whey protein isolate, unflavored

STOP

VEGETARIAN PROTEINS:
Fried eggs 💧💧💧
Fried tofu 💧💧💧
Whey protein isolated, flavored

MEAT & FISH: GO	
1/2 can (60g)	Canned tuna, in water
70g raw	Chicken or turkey, white, no skin
80g raw	Lobster
80g raw	Crab
230g (16) raw	Oysters
80g raw	White fish, cod, sole, haddock, tilapia...
75g raw	Game meats, horse, bison, deer, caribou
70g raw	Pork, tenderloin
80g raw (12 large)	Shrimp and scallops

MEAT & FISH:	
1/2 can (60g)	Canned tuna, in oil drained 💧
75g raw	Liver, chicken, veal, pork, beef 💧
90g raw	Chicken, thighs, dark meat 💧
80g raw	Fatty fish, salmon, herring, sardines, mackerel 💧
90g raw	Ground turkey, chicken, pork 💧
75g raw	Pork loin 💧
90g raw	Ground beef, extra lean or lean 💧💧
70g raw	Beef, sirloin, round, loin 💧💧
90g raw	Veal, cutlet, loin, sirloin, minced, stewed 💧💧
80g raw	Lamb, ribs 💧💧

MEAT & FISH: STOP	
2 slices (70g)	Deli meats, turkey, chicken, ham 💧
150g	Smoked salmon 💧
90g raw	Pork spare ribs 💧💧💧
1 1/2	Hot dogs 💧💧💧
100g	Raw lamb, loin, tenderloin, shoulder 💧💧💧
13 slices	Pepperoni, salami, bologna 💧💧💧
110g raw	Beef ribs 💧💧💧
80g raw	Sausage, italian, merguez, pork 💧💧💧
140g raw	Duck meat and skin 💧💧💧

DIG DEEPER 4: MEAL PLANS FOR DIFFERENT SITUATIONS

Family Friendly Meal Plans

The following sample meal plans will give you an idea of how to increase your performance in hockey by planning meals and snacks around different hockey situations.

If there are some foods or snacks in the meal plans that you don't like, use the Stoplight Guides in the Digging Deeper section or the list of Energizer Snacks (Chapter 30) to replace them.

Do you want more meal plans, delicious recipes and a travel meal planner?

Check out the online Active Family Meal Planner program by SOS Cuisine & Eat This for Performance in Hockey

SITUATION 1: SCHOOLDAY / HOCKEY 9 PM

Breakfast:

- Waffles with fresh strawberries and maple syrup
- Peanut butter
- Milk or soymilk
- Fruit juice

AM snack:

- Granola bar
- Water

Lunch:

- Egg salad sandwich
- Radish and cucumber salad with dressing

PHOTO: SOSCUISINE.COM

Try SOS CUISINE.com's meal planner tools for hockey families

- Water

Dinner (6 pm):

- Barbecue pulled chicken sandwich (see recipe)
- Apple compote
- Milk or soymilk

Pre-hockey fuel and hydration (between 7 pm and 9 pm):

- Drink water often without over-hydrating
- If needed: snack from the Energizer Snack list (Chapter 30)
- If needed: Have a Quick Energizer Snack such as a sports drink or a homemade sports drink (recipe Chapter 33)

HOCKEY AT 9 PM:

- Drink water every 15 minutes, drink sports drinks if needed

Post-hockey recovery snack (in the locker room):

- Greek yogourt
- Almonds
- Raisins

Post-hockey hydration:

- In the 4-6 hours after hockey drink water regularly to replace weight lost from sweating

Barbecue pulled chicken sandwich

PHOTO: SOSCUISINE.COM

Recipe part of the online Active Family Meal Planner program by SOS Cuisine & Eat This for Performance in Hockey

14 chicken thighs, boneless, skinless
6 drops Tabasco sauce
2 jalapeño pepper, fresh, chopped
4 tsp white vinegar
1/2 tbsp honey
1 3/4 tsp paprika
2 tsp mustard powder
1 onion, finely chopped
4 cloves garlic, minced
1 cup strained tomatoes
2 tbsp canola oil
6 panino rolls
6 tomatoes, sliced

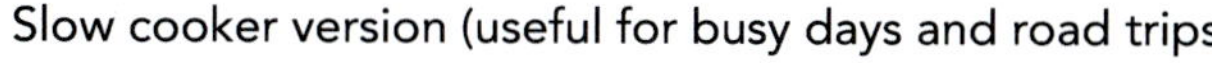

Slow cooker version (useful for busy days and road trips)

1. Put all the ingredients, but bread and tomato, in the ceramic

cooking pot. Mix well.

2. Cover the slow cooker with the lid and cook on 'high' for 3-4 h, or until the chicken meat is tender enough to be "pulled" apart easily with a fork. Once cooked, remove the chicken from the slow cooker and pull apart with two forks. Add the chicken back to the slow cooker then mix well.
3. Serve the chicken in panini buns and garnish with sliced tomatoes.

SITUATION 2: SCHOOLDAY / HOCKEY AT 7 PM

Breakfast:

- Whole grain cereal and milk
- Kiwi
- Fruit Juice

AM snack:

- Orange
- Peanut butter and crackers
- Water

PHOTO: SOSCUISINE.COM

Lunch:

- Fresh mozzarella and tomato sandwich
- Carrot and celery sticks with dip
- Water

Dinner (5 pm):

Smaller portion like the Light Hockey Player's Plate (Chapter 10)

- Pesto Pasta with Tuna (see recipe)

Pre-hockey fuel and hydration (between 5 pm and 7 pm):

- Drink water often without over-hydrating
- If needed: snack from the Energizer Snack list (Chapter 30)
- If needed: Have a Quick Energizer Snack such as a sports drink or a homemade sports drink (recipe Chapter 33)

HOCKEY AT 7 PM:

- Drink water every 15 minutes, drink sports drinks if needed

Post-hockey recovery snack (in the locker room):

- Smoothie
- Nuts
- Milk or soymilk

Post-hockey hydration:

- In the 4-6 hours after hockey drink water regularly to replace weight lost from sweating

Bedtime snack (time permitting):

- Pretzels and peanuts
- Water
- Banana

Pesto Pasta with Tuna for 4

PHOTO: SOSCUISINE.COM

Recipe part of the online Active Family Meal Planner program by SOS Cuisine & Eat This for Performance in Hockey

4 cups penne rigate, or other short pasta
200 grams tuna, canned, in vegetable oil, drained and shredded
1/2 cup pesto sauce
3 tbsp lemon juice, freshly squeezed

3 tbsp olive oil
1/2 cup pasta cooking water, approximately

1. To save time, the sauce preparation and the pasta cooking can be done at the same time. Start cooking the pasta.
2. Open the tuna can, then drain and discard the oil. Shred the tuna then add it to a bowl. Stir in the pesto sauce, lemon juice, olive oil, and enough of the pasta cooking water to make a sauce. Mix well, then adjust the seasoning. Generally, you don't need to add salt since tuna is already salty.
3. Pour the drained pasta into the serving bowl and mix thoroughly with the sauce. Serve in the warmed dishes.

SITUATION 3: WEEKEND TOURNAMENT / GAMES AT 8 AM & 2 PM

*increase intake of carbohydrate-rich snacks 3 days prior to tournament

Bedtime snack (the night before):

- Low fat cheddar cheese melted on a bagel
- Apple
- Water

Breakfast (before 6:30 am):

- Fruit smoothie
- Rice cakes

DIG DEEPER

Pre-game fuel and hydration (between 6 am and 8 am):

- Drink water often without over-hydrating
- If needed: snack from the Energizer Snack list (Chapter 30)
- If needed: Have a Quick Energizer Snack such as a sports drink or a homemade sports drink (recipe Chapter 33)

GAME AT 8 AM:

- Drink water every 15 minutes, drink sports drinks if needed

Post-game recovery snack (in the locker room):

- Granola bar
- Chocolate milk
- Water

Lunch (11 am):

- Spaghetti
- Meat sauce
- Fresh fruit salad
- Water

Pre-game fuel and hydration (between 12 pm and 2 pm):

- Drink water often without over-hydrating
- If needed: snack from the Energizer Snack list (Chapter 30)
- If needed: Have a Quick Energizer Snack such as a sports drink or a homemade sports drink (recipe Chapter 33)

GAME AT 2 PM:

- Drink water every 15 minutes, drink sports drinks if needed

Post-game recovery snack (in the locker room):

- Milk or soymilk
- Banana

Post-game hydration:

- In the 4-6 hours after hockey drink water regularly to replace weight lost from sweating

Dinner:

- Performance Stew (see recipe)
- Water

Bedtime snack:

- Boiled egg
- Toast or crackers
- Water

Try SOS CUISINE.com's meal planner tools for hockey families

Performance Stew for 6

PHOTO: SOSCUISINE.COM

Recipe part of the online Active Family Meal Planner program by SOS Cuisine & Eat This for Performance in Hockey

750 g stewing beef cubes, of about 2 cm
1/2 cup white flour (all purpose)
1/4 cup canola oil
6 cloves garlic, minced
4 cups beef broth
3 tbsp tomato paste
1 1/2 tbsp sugar
1 1/2 tbsp Worcestershire sauce
1 sprig rosemary, fresh
3 bay leaf
1 ½ onions, coarsely chopped
3 stalks celery, cut into 1 cm pieces
7 ½ potatoes, peeled then cut into 1 cm pieces
3 carrots, peeled then cut into 1 cm pieces
3 tbsp butter, unsalted
3 tbsp Italian parsley, fresh, chopped

1. Cut the beef into 2 cm cubes, if not already cubed, then dredge the cubes in flour.
2. Heat the oil in a large pot over medium-high heat. Add the beef cubes and sauté until they are browned on all sides, about 5-6 min. Mince the garlic, then add it to the pot. Add the broth, tomato paste, sugar, Worcestershire sauce, rosemary sprig(s), and bay leaves. Stir to combine. Bring the mixture to a boil, then reduce the heat to medium-low, cover and simmer 1 h, stirring occasionally.
3. Meanwhile, prepare the vegetables : coarsely chop the onions; cut the celery stalks into 1 cm pieces; peel the potatoes and carrots, then cut them into 1 cm pieces.
4. Melt the butter in another large pot over medium heat. Add the vegetables and sauté until they are golden, about 20 min, with occasional stirring. Add the vegetables to the beef stew. Continue to simmer, uncovered, until the beef and vegetables are very tender, about 40 min. Season with salt and pepper. Discard the bay leaves and rosemary sprig(s), sprinkle with the chopped parsley, then serve.

(*) If the stew is too liquid, remove some of the excess broth and serve it separately as a soup.

SITUATION 4: WEEKEND / HOCKEY AT 2 PM

Breakfast (before 9 am):

- Oatmeal
- Fresh blueberries
- Almonds
- Milk or soymilk

Lunch (11:30 am):

- Pasta with tuna, carrot and celery
- Tapioca pudding
- Water

Pre-hockey fuel and hydration (between 12 pm and 2 pm):

- Drink water often without over-hydrating
- If needed: snack from the Energizer Snack list (Chapter 30)
- If needed: Have a Quick Energizer Snack such as a sports drink or a homemade sports drink (recipe Chapter 33)

HOCKEY AT 2 PM:

Drink water every 15 minutes, drink sports drinks if needed

Post-hockey recovery snack (in the locker room):

- Turkey sandwich
- Orange slices

Post-hockey hydration:

- In the 4-6 hours after hockey drink water regularly to replace weight lost from sweating

Afternoon snack:

- Cut fresh veggies and hummus
- Pera slices
- Milk or soymilk

Dinner:

- Performance quiches (see recipe)
- Parsley and whole grain couscous salad with walnuts
- Frozen yogourt and fresh berries

Performance Quiches for 3

Recipe part of the online Active Family Meal Planner program by SOS Cuisine & Eat This for Performance in Hockey

PHOTO: SOSCUISINE.COM

vegetable oil spray, for the muffin tin
1 cup brown rice
2 cups chicken broth
2/3 cup milk, partly skimmed, 2%
3/4 cup evaporated milk powder
1 cup Cheddar cheese, shredded
6 eggs size large
1 clove garlic, finely chopped
2 tsp herbes de Provence

Preheat the oven to 175°C/350°F. Spray a 6-cup muffin pan with a vegetable oil spray. Cook the rice in the broth, about 30 min.

In a large bowl, whisk the eggs, milk and milk powder using a fork. Stir in cheese, garlic and herbes de Provence, then mix well. Spoon the cooked rice into the cups of the muffin pan. Press the rice lightly to the bottom of each cup, so that it forms a crust. Fill the muffin cups with the egg mixture.

Bake in the middle of the oven for about 25-30 min, until a toothpick inserted into the center of a muffin comes out clean. Take the pan out of the oven, leave to cool for a few minutes. Serve 2 mini-quiches per person.

SITUATION 5: WEEKEND / HOCKEY AT 4 PM

Breakfast (before 9 am):

- Whole grain toast and eggs
- Cantaloupe
- Yogourt
- Orange Juice

AM snack:

- Pear

Try SOS CUISINE.com's meal planner tools for hockey families

- Oatmeal cookies (low fat)

Lunch (before 1 pm):

- Peak Lasagna (see recipe)
- Toast
- Tomato and cucumber salad with dressing
- Water

Pre-hockey fuel and hydration (between 2 pm and 4 pm):

- Drink water often without over-hydrating
- If needed: snack from the Energizer Snack list (Chapter 30)
- If needed: Have a Quick Energizer Snack such as a sports drink or a homemade sports drink (recipe Chapter 33)

HOCKEY AT 4 PM:

- Drink water every 15 minutes, drink sports drinks if needed

Post-hockey recovery snack (in the locker room):

- Milk or soymilk

Post-hockey hydration:

- In the 4-6 hours after hockey drink water regularly to replace weight lost from sweating

Dinner:

- Athlete meatballs (see recipe)
- Mixed dark lettuce and strawberry salad
- Chocolate pudding

Bedtime snack:

- Cereal and milk or soymilk
- Fruit juice

Peak Lasagna for 6

PHOTO: SOSCUISINE.COM

Recipe part of the online Active Family Meal Planner program by SOS Cuisine & Eat This for Performance in Hockey

1 small butternut squash
1 cup white "navy" beans (canned), rinsed
3 tbsp canola oil
2 3/4 cups ricotta cheese, light
8 cups baby spinach, chopped
1 cup fresh basil, finely chopped
1 pinch nutmeg
1/2 tbsp dried oregano
3 tbsp olive oil
20 lasagne noodles, oven-ready type
1 1/2 cup mozzarella cheese, grated

Cook the squash Preheat the oven to 190°C/375°F.

Cut the squash in half lengthwise, remove the seeds. Place the halves on a baking sheet, cut side down. Bake about 45-50 min until soft. Alternatively, cook each halve separately in a microwave oven: Place each halve in a bowl, partially covered, then cook at high intensity about 8 min for each halve. Let the halves cool down and carve out the pulp.

Assemble the lasagna Combine squash, white beans, canola oil, salt and pepper in a food processor and purée until smooth. Set aside. In a large bowl, combine ricotta, spinach, half of the basil and the other seasonings. Mix well and set aside. Using a brush, generously coat a 6-quart or larger slow cooker with olive oil.

Arrange a layer of noodles as the base of the lasagna in the slow cooker. Spread half of the squash mixture in the slow cooker. Arrange another layer noodles over the squash mixture, overlapping them slightly. Spread the ricotta mixture over the noodles and firmly pat down, then arrange a layer of noodles over the ricotta mixture, breaking into pieces to cover as much as possible. Spoon on remaining squash mixture. Finish with a layer of noodles and cover with grated mozzarella. Cook

Put the lid on the slow cooker and cook on 'High' for 3-4 h. Sprinkle the remaining basil on the lasagna then serve.

PHOTO: SOSCUISINE.COM

Athlete Meatballs

Recipe part of the online Active Family Meal Planner program by SOS Cuisine & Eat This for Performance in Hockey

1 tbsp canola oil
1 1/2 slice bread, whole wheat, stale or day-old
2 cups tomato sauce
40 g mortadella sausage, or ham , finely chopped
1 tbsp marjoram, fresh, finely chopped
1 large egg
400 g ground beef, extra-lean
3 tbsp bread crumbs
260 g fettuccine
2 tsp extra virgin olive oil

Preheat the oven to 205°C/400°F and lightly grease a baking dish with the canola oil.

Put the bread slices in a small bowl then cover them with water (you may need to put a weight on top to submerge the slices). Let soak 20-30 min. Meanwhile, warm up the tomato sauce in a large pan over low heat.

Drain the bread well in a sieve, then squeeze it to remove most of the liquid. Finely chop the bread then add it to a bowl. Finely chop the mortadella (or ham) and marjoram, then add them to the bowl. Add the egg and ground beef, followed by salt and pepper to taste. Using your hands, blend the mixture together until it is just combined well (do not overmix). Form the mixture into small balls (about the size of golf balls), then flatten them slightly and coat them with the bread crumbs. Plan on about 3-4 meatballs per serving. Transfer the meatballs to the previously oiled dish, then cook in the middle of the oven 12-15 min until they are golden-brown, turning them once. Transfer the meatballs to the pan with the tomato sauce then continue to cook 15-20 min over medium-low heat, turning them once.

Meanwhile, cook the pasta. Put the drained fettuccine immediately back in the pasta cooking pot with the extra virgin olive oil. Mix well then serve with the meatballs and sauce.

Go to: www.EatThisForPerformance.com/Hockey

FOR ALL LINKS TO ONLINE DOCUMENTS, PROGRAMS, and UPDATES!

DIG DEEPER 5: THE NUTRITION EDGE HOCKEY BAG KITS

Make sure you are always able to get a nutrition edge by packing your hockey bag full of snack kits. Here are three kits that are hockey bag proof and can stay in the hockey bag for weeks without making your bag smell (smell more, that is!). And, if you are craving fresh snacks, choose some of the fresh options to pack for the day along with your kit.

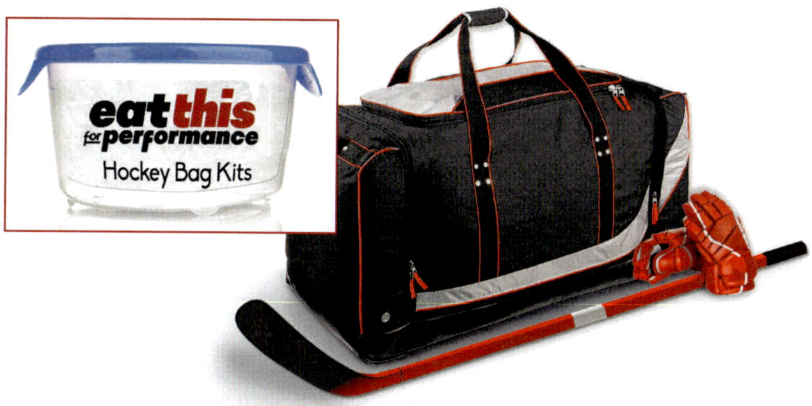

KIT 1:	Quick Edge Muffin Recipe:
Quick edge muffin mixes Applesauces Dried apricots Almonds UHT (ultra heat treated) chocolate milk 	Mix at home: 3 tbsp (45ml) quick cooking oats, 1 tbsp (15ml) wheat germ, 2 tbsp flour(30ml), 1/8 tsp (0.5ml) baking soda, 1 tbsp raisins (15ml), 1 tsp (5ml) brown sugar, 1/4 tsp (1ml) cinnamon, 3 tbsp (45ml) skim milk At the rink: add 3 tbsp (45ml) applesauce to the dry ingredients and mix, put batterin a mug or a silicon cup and microwave on high for 1 minute. Let the muffin sit for 2 minutes.

KIT 2:

Cereal (granola or oat cereal)
Skim milk powder
Power cookies

Power Cookies Recipe:

9 Graham crackers crushed
1/4 cup raisins
3 tbsp peanut butter natural, or almond butter
2 tbsp honey
1 tbsp water
2 tbsp unsweetened coconut flakes

Combined the crushed graham crackers with the rest of the ingredients, except coconut, then mix well. Pat mixture into 8 cookies and press lightly in coconut.

KIT 3:

Quick edge couscous mixes
UHT (ultra-heat-treated) milk
Crackers
Almond butter

Quick Edge Couscous Recipe:

1/4 cup couscous, whole wheat
1 tsp chicken stock powder
2 tbsp evaporated milk powder
7 dried apricots
3 tbsp slivered almonds
1/4 cup water

Microwave on high for 1 min and let sit for 5 minutes.

Fresh Items to Pack:

- Greek yogurt
- Cheese
- Fresh fruit
- Fresh vegetables
- Hummus

Suggested Hardware to Use:

- Microwavable container
- Shake mixer
- Ingredient bags for dry ingredients

DIG DEEPER 6: THE SUPPLEMENT SUPPLEMENT

Supplements are not needed for most teen athletes, no matter if they are national calibre or playing for fun. The Top Performance Pyramid (Chapter 16) shows just how little supplements contribute to performance. But, we didn't want you to be without information on supplements. So in case you are curious about the supplement world, we have included some more detailed information about supplements here.

There are 4 types of supplements:

A. Nutrients you cannot get in your diet or cannot absorb easily.

B. Nutrients that boost what you get from food.

C. Non-nutrient substances that are commonly eaten and not banned for use in sport.

D. Sports Foods.

A. Nutrients you cannot get in your diet or cannot absorb easily: If you are following a strict diet such as the vegan diet you will need to check if a supplement is important to make sure you are not creating a deficiency or limiting your performance. Chapter 14 talks about diets and what to watch out for. Usually a blood test will be needed to determine if you are not absorbing the nutrients from food properly. The blood tests are not able to check for everything. To date, there are very accurate and commonly available blood tests for iron, folate, vitamin B12, and vitamin D. If you are deficient in a nutrient you will work your medical team to evaluate why you are deficient and correct the deficit. Vitamin D is special because it happens to be a vitamin that many indoor athletes are deficient in. Read the vitamin D section in this supplement.

B. Sports foods: These are processed foods or drinks that replace or supplement your diet when you are playing your sport or close to playing your sport. You will not find these foods growing in nature, they have gone through several steps to remove all the nutrients except a few. For example, cane sugar came from the sugar cane plant but the end product that is used in a sports food is pure sugar with none if the plant's fibres and other minerals. Sports foods are not everyday foods, but they can be useful if you are not able to meet all of your nutritional needs with foods and drinks that come from unprocessed plants and animals. Sports Foods tend to have added colours and artificial flavours along with the nutrient of interest. If you experience a reaction to a sport food check to see that it is not just a reaction to that particular flavour and colour.

C. Nutrients that can boost the amount of that nutrient your body gets from food: You might be eating a well balanced diet and performing very well but wondering if you could boost your performance just a little. That is when you know you are ready to try proven supplements. According to recent research on hockey players and similar sports, Creatine, Beta-Alanine, Casein, Beet Juice, Multivitamins, Gelatin and fish oil may be interesting supplements to enhance performance. Make sure to get professional advice from a qualified sports dietitian before launching into a supplement program. Get guidance to select the supplement, decide on when and how much to take and for how long you will take that supplement. There is a reason it takes at least 6 years to complete an advanced nutrition degree - nutrition is not something you can pick up overnight!

D. Non-nutrient substances that are commonly eaten and not banned for use in sport: Both caffeine and probiotics are substances that are not nutrients but both have proven positive effects for athletes. Read on to learn more about them. Again, make sure to get professional advice from a qualified sports dietitian before launching into a supplement program.

Sports dietitians are trained to guide you in the use of supplements. There are also some good research summaries on supplements available on the Australian Institute of Sports website (www.ausport.gov.au/ais/nutrition). If reading about supplements is confusing you, make sure you take a session with a sports dietitian to ask all your questions.

VITAMIN AND MINERAL SUPPLEMENTS

Vitamins and minerals are always considered supplements (NOT replacements), meaning they are taken in addition to food. Pills or foods with added vitamins and minerals should never be considered a replacement for bad nutrition habits. Sports dietitians will work individually with a hockey player to assess if a vitamin or mineral supplement is needed. The good news is that a balanced and varied diet will provide the 23 vitamins and minerals that need to be consumed. It is harder to get enough of some vitamins and minerals. Does that mean that you will need to take a supplement? No. Most of the time, all that is needed is to eat more of certain vitamin - and mineral-rich foods. The hockey players' sports dietitian and sports medicine doctor will use complex assessments before recommending a vitamin or mineral supplement.

What vitamins and minerals should I ask my sports dietitian about?

Everyone should ask about:	Vegetarians should ask about:
• Vitamin D	• Iron • Calcium • Vitamin D • Riboflavin • Zinc • Vitamin B12
Heavy sweaters should ask about:	**Picky eaters and those with a lot of food allergies should ask about:**
• Sodium • Potassium • Magnesium • Calcium	• Multivitamins

WATCH OUT!

There are some vitamins and minerals that could decrease performance of a hockey player if they have too much. Do not fall into the trap of thinking more is better. More is not better when it comes to vitamins and minerals.

THE MAXIMUM AMOUNT A 14 TO 18-YEAR-OLD SHOULD TAKE (INDICATED IN BRACKETS)

- Vitamin D (4000 IU)

  Form 1: Cholecalciferol (D3)*

  Form 2: Ergocalciferol (D2)
- Vitamin E (800 mg)
- Vitamin A (2800 mcg)
- Vitamin C (1800 mg)
- Niacin (30 mg)
- Vitamin B6 (80 mg)
- Folate (800 mcg)
- Choline (3000 mg)
- Iron (45 mg of elemental iron)

  Form 1: Ferrous Gluconate has 35mg of elemental iron per 300mg dose

  Form 2: Ferrous Sulfate has 60mg of elemental iron per 300mg dose
- Calcium (3000 mg)

  Form 1: Calcium Carbonate

  Form 2: Calcium Citrate (recommended form)
- Sodium (2300 mg)
- Magnesium (350 mg)
- Phosphorous (4000 mg)
- Zinc (34 mg)
- Fluoride (10 mg)
- Selenium (400 mcg)
- Copper (8000 mcg)
- Iodine (900 mcg)
- Manganese (9 mg)

* Vitamin D3 is found in animal sources and is made from UV rays (sunlight). D3 is more effective at raising vitamin D levels in the blood. There are studies which show that the D3 form is preferred for supplementation.

SPORTS GELS AND SPORTS CANDIES

They look like candy, but they will taste slightly salty. You can use these products instead of foods in between periods or close to a game or practice if food upsets your stomach. The benefit of taking a sport gel or sport candy is that is does not contain fibre like whole foods generally do. Fibre can slow down digestion of a food. You should look for 15 to 30 gram portions of carbohydrate. Be careful to avoid the products with caffeine unless you are following the advice of a sports dietitian.

MEAL REPLACEMENTS (DRINKS, SPORTS BARS)

Meal replacements are not perfect substitutes for real food, and they will not give you the nutrition edge over the competition. However, there may be some times when a meal is just not possible and a meal replacement bar or drink is better than many fast food options. A meal replacement is a much better option than skipping a meal altogether.

Meal Replacement:	ENERGY	PROTEIN	CARBS	FAT
PowerBar®	200	9	43	1.6
PowerBar® Protein Plus™	210	20	26	5
PowerBar® Triple Threat®	225	10	28	8
PowerBar® Harvest® Bar	216	10	34	4.8
Clif® Bar (chocolate brownie)	230	9	44	4.5
Clif® Bar Builder's® (chocolate)	270	20	30	8
Vega One Nutritional Shake™	141	15	13	3.3
Boost®	240	10	41	4
Boost® High Protein	240	15	33	6
Boost Plus®	360	14	45	14
Gatorade Recover®	120	16	14	0
Ensure® (milk chocolate)	250	9	40	6
Ensure® Plus (milk chocolate)	350	13	50	11
Ensure® Muscle Health (milk chocolate)	250	13	32	8
Ensure® Complete™ (milk chocolate)	350	13	52	11
Ensure® High Protein (milk chocolate)	210	25	23	2.5

SPORT DRINKS

Sports drinks are special mixes of water, sugar, and salt. The amount of each ingredient that is used allows most hockey players to replace their sweat and replenish their energy stores (batteries!) without getting an upset stomach. Sports drinks are meant for use during activity (not before or after). You can usually digest sugar while you play. For practices and games longer than 1 hour, the extra energy provided can improve performance. If the percent of sugar is too high in the drink (more than 8 per cent), you could get an upset stomach. If the sodium levels are too high (greater than 175mg per 250ml), the taste of the drink is affected and you might not drink it because it tastes salty. Since it is generally not possible to get back all of the sodium that is lost while playing hockey by using sports drinks, you should replenish your sodium in your post-training drinks, snacks, and meals.

Here are some common brand names hockey players will see:

Sports Drink:	SUGAR %	SODIUM (Salt) mg/250ml
Gatorade® Perform®	6%	105mg
G2®	2%	115mg
Powerade®	6%	100mg
Biosteel® [1]	0%	78.5mg
Cytomax® [2]	7%	100mg
Isostar®	6%	120mg
All Sport®	7%	55mg
Other Drinks:		
O.N.E.™ Coconut water plain	4%	49mg
O.N.E.™ Coconut water flavoured[3]	7%	115-130mg

1. 6.25g of powder mixed with 250ml of water

2. 25g of powder mixed with 300ml of water

3. Watch out! A source of dietary fibre (1g per 250ml).

PROTEIN POWDERS

You can easily get the necessary protein you need in a day by eating regular foods. For example, eating 2 eggs, 2 ounces (60 grams) of cheese, 175g of yogurt, a glass of milk, and 1 chicken breast along with a good amount of grains at each meal will be sufficient to get 100 grams of protein. If food options are not available, a protein powder can replace a food on occasion. A protein powder is concentrated, therefore a small scoop is often enough to replace one of the food proteins. Protein powders can be helpful when they are taken in the right amount, at the right time, and are made by the right company. So, how does someone know what is right for them? Hockey players should have guidance from a sports dietitian to answer this question. Products that are certified for use in sport are the most reliable products. Companies that provide health care facilities with protein powder are often reliable and can also be good options for athletes. Unfortunately, most protein powders sold are not certified and may not contain safe ingredients. Another consideration is that protein powders do not replace whole protein sources perfectly and some athletes experience bloating and stomach upset with too much processed protein powder.

TYPES OF PROTEIN POWDERS

Protein powders originally come from food. Most hockey players will have had all of the following protein powders in food form already.

1. Whey protein is the most common protein powder sold. Whey comes from animal milks, usually cow's milk. Some whey proteins will say "Whey Protein Isolate." Whey protein isolate is just a fancy way of saying that this whey protein does not have any of the other stuff found in milk (sugars, fats, cholesterol, vitamins or minerals) whereas other whey protein powders will have some leftover stuff, often cholesterol.

2. Casein protein also comes from animal milks, usually cow's milk. This protein has been found to pass more slowly through the digestive system making it an interesting protein source to have consumed before sleep. The ability to build muscle while you sleep is being explored with casein protein.

3. Soy protein is a popular plant based protein powder. It comes from the soybean.

4. Pea protein is becoming more popular. This protein comes from peas.

5. Amino acids are the building blocks of protein. Hockey players have been targeted by supplement companies to try branch chain amino acids, beta-alanine, glutamine, and taurine among

others. It is important to know that amino acids like these are only a part of proteins. If you eat protein, you are eating many amino acids - which is good, because your body needs different amino acids to build muscle protein. If a sports dietitian decides a protein powder is the right choice for a hockey player, they first assess the other protein sources the hockey player is eating in their diet to see which protein powder will give the hockey player the right balance of amino acids. Taking a single amino acid supplement is not the same as taking a protein supplement, and an expert sports dietitian will be needed to guide the hockey player.

PROBIOTICS

Probiotics are friendly bacteria that can live in your digestive system. To get probiotics, you need to make sure you are eating living bacteria, not dead ones. Heat destroys bacteria, and most products are pasteurized to kill all bacteria for your safety (so you do not eat bad bacteria!). Some foods, such as some yogurts, cheese, and other milk products, will be pasteurized first, then good bacteria will be added back to the food. Check the label to see how many bacteria you can get in 1 serving. Most athletes will be able to tolerate 2 billion bacteria per day. The food sources of probiotic bacteria are useful because you get food PLUS probiotics. Having the food at the same time as the bacteria keeps the bacteria healthy. Probiotics should be started in small doses and taken at the same time each day. Amounts should be increased gradually. Eating too many probiotics too quickly may cause gas, bloating and stomach pain.

FISH OIL

Fish oil comes from the fat of cold-water fish. Fish oil contains essential fats called Omega-3's that your body cannot make and therefore you need to eat. In addition, fish oil has interesting anti-inflammatory effects. There are two main types of omega-3 fatty acids: Long-chain omega-3 fatty acids are EPA (eicosapentaenoic acid) and DHA (docosahexaenoic acid). Short-chain omega-3 fatty acids are ALA (alpha-linolenic acid). These are found in plants, such as flaxseed. So far research on ALA omega-3 fatty acids shows that they have less benefits than EPA and DHA. Health Canada recommends eating at least 2 servings of fish per week (75 g or 2

1/2 oz.). Each serving provides an average of about 0.3-0.45 grams of DHA or EPA per day. Fish: Salmon, Mackerel, Sardines, Herring, Arctic Char, Anchovies, and Trout. If you are not meeting your recommendations you should discuss fish oil supplementation with a sports dietitian.

BEETROOT JUICE (NITRATE-RICH JUICE)

Beetroot juice has recently been studied because of its high nitrate content. Recent research has discovered that nitrates can have positive health effects. Taking large amounts of beetroot juice as a supplement may be helpful for performance once your diet is optimal. Some non-harmful side-effects have been reported including bright red coloured urine! Talk to your sports RD to find out if you might benefit from taking beetroot juice supplements. However, it should be noted that recent evidence is linking foods high in nitrates with the same performance benefits as the juice version. So eating your veggies has now gotten that much more interesting! Here is a list of high-nitrate foods which you are encouraged to eat regularly:

- Beetroots
- Celery
- Arugula (a type of small leaf lettuce)
- Cress (a type of sprout greens)

CREATINE

Simply put creatine is how your body gets energy in the first seconds of a sprint - it is the helper that quickly taps into your energy stores when you need it in a pinch. Active people, athletes, injured, the elderly are all going to benefit from having muscles filled with creatine. But should you supplement? Only a maybe here. It's hard to say if it's worth the trouble and the expense without looking at your exact situation. Here are two examples of when an augmented creatine volume in your muscles might give you a boost: If you eat a vegan or meat-less diet and if you are training in high heat and want to stay more hydrated.

Who should NOT take creatine: Anyone who is not sure their diet

is optimized for getting benefits from the creatine supplement.

A MINI "HOW-TO" (DO NOT JUST FOLLOW THIS PLAN AS IT'S NOT YOUR PLAN)

How Josh is taking Creatine Monohydrate
Josh weighs 165lbs, he is a lean 15 year old hockey players who eats a super diet containing the muscle builders, superfoods, and energizers. His diet and hydration strategies are optimized through careful testing of pre-hockey meals, snacks, and breakfasts. He is ready to take creatine with guidance of his sports RD. Here is the way he was instructed to take it:

Step 1: He purchased a certified creatine monohydrate supplement.

Step 2: He tried 1 small dose of creatine supplement at supper on an off-day to make sure he would not react negatively to taking the supplement.

Step 3: For 5 days he put the powder into his food or drink at his three meals and one snack in his day. He took a teaspoon to measure 5 grams of powder per meal.

Step 4: On day 6 he started to only take the creatine supplement at breakfast until his next meeting with his sports RD.

GELATIN

Gelatin is a food derivative of collagen. Collagen has been described by some as the support structure of your body. Like a house has support beams that hold up the roof, you have collagen that holds your tendons, ligaments, and muscles together. Increased collagen has been linked to injury prevention, recovery from injury, and recovery from workouts. Research on athletes is promising and we recommend keeping an eye on this supplement for use in your diet in the future.

CAFFEINE

Caffeine is a naturally occurring stimulant found in coffee beans, chocolate, tea, guarana, yerba mate and other plants. People supplement with caffeine for sports performance to reduce the perception of exercise being hard. There are studies proving caffeine stimulation does slightly boost athletic performance. However, the dose needed is small, and the amount of caffeine in natural sources is unknown which makes it hard to take the right amount. We recommend you use a known amount of caffeine when using caffeine as a performance enhancer - so that means non-natural sources. We also do not necessarily recommend caffeine for hockey games. This is because many elite level hockey games are played in the evening. Caffeine can have stimulant effects that will last for hours after the game and may disrupt sleep. Sleep has greater performance benefits than caffeine so ideally you would choose sleep over caffeine supplementation.

BETA-ALANINE

Beta-alanine (B-alanine) is an amino acid (part of muscle builders) used to increase muscle carnosine. Carnosine sometimes gets confused with carnitine but they are not the same. Carnosine is a helper in relieving muscle fatigue as it soaks up the acidic build up from your hard working muscles. Hockey players, because they do a sprint sport, and people who have a high protein diet already have high amounts of muscle carnosine. Vegans and vegetarians may want to supplement with beta-alanine. But, like creatine, your diet should be optimized before starting on beta-alanine. There is also a special protocol (way to take a supplement) that we use with b-alanine. Some small uncomfortable side-effects can be avoided this way.

Some supplements are known to be dangerous and harmful to athletic performance. AVOID the following supplements if you want to be healthy:

- ***Secret "proprietary" blends (where they don't tell you exactly how much of each ingredient is in the product)***
- ***Fat loss pills or powders sometimes known as "fat burners"***
- ***Energizer drinks, pills, or powders***
- ***Supplements with claims that seem too good to be true***
- ***Stimulants: ephedrine, strychnine, sibutramine, and methyhexanamine***
- ***Steroids, otherwise known as prohormones and hormone boosters: DHEA, androstenedione, 19-norandrostenione***

Need more information on how to take supplements? Get with the programs offered by Eat This for Performance in Hockey. www.eatthisforperformance.com/hockey

DIG DEEPER 7: DIGGING DEEPER INTO PERIODIZATION

Periodization in sport describes planned strategies in exercise or nutrition that intend to give the athlete a better result than if periodized strategies were not used. Sometimes the strategies will be planned for a long time period (weeks) and sometimes only for a short time period (hours).

PERIODIZING EXERCISE

If you always do the exact same workout routine, your body will adapt to the stimulus and will not be as challenged. It is well recognized that changing a workout routine after a period of time can lead to quicker fitness results. This could be change in type of exercise (strength VS endurance), change in duration of exercise (seconds VS hours), or change in intensity of exercise (high VS low). There is a lot of interest in having young elite hockey players involved in multiple sports for a long time before specializing in their chosen sport in part for the periodization effect on musculoskeletal development.

PERIODIZING NUTRITION

The idea of periodizing nutrition is both old and new. Old, because we have been naturally periodizing our eating habits without giving it a name. For example, when we eat more of a particular fruit that is in-season or when we eat a later breakfast on the weekend we are changing our food intake to a different routine. The new aspect of nutritional periodization comes from research that can explain how some of these natural habits may work for us or against us. What scientists may be calling new discoveries are actually probably just good explanations to what athletes have been doing by accident using trial and error!

If you eat to fuel your exercise like we recommend in this book, then you will need to have a different eating strategy to match each change in your activity level. Match your periodizations in food intake to periodizations planned in your exercise programs. If you eat at a lot of energizers one week and need to decrease your intake to go with a lighter week of hockey the next week, then you are periodizing your energy intake.

Known as "Carb Loading": Periodizing carbs for events
Playing in an elite level game with 20 minute periods that could go into overtime? Playing in a 3-day tournament? In preparation for events lasting longer than 90 minutes or for tournament situations when eating large meals in between events will be difficult, supercharging your batteries can improve performance. The supercharging starts 36 to 48 hours before the event. Chances are that carbohydrate loading or "supercharging" your muscles with carbs will help make sure you perform well.

At one time, carbohydrate loading involved a complicated system of carbohydrate cutting and intense exercising and then eating a high-carb diet so that muscles could generate a supercharge. However research has clarified that simply eating more carbohydrate (about 8 to 12 grams per kg of your body weight per day) and training less in the 2 to 3 days before your event, will provide a performance enhancing supercharge.

The new buzz: Periodizing carbs in training
There is a lot of buzz and misunderstanding around carbs. Even though we know that hockey players need carbs for energy (see Chapter 1), there are some good studies on athletes showing that a carb-free muscle might be more stimulated around exercise to be better at using fat as fuel during endurance competitions. Not sprint competitions. We are very clearly talking about endurance sports - usually involving longer than 90 minutes of constant movement. Why would you want to be better at using fat as fuel during endurance competitions? First, because fat is so abundant and second, if you can spare some carbohydrate energy at the beginning of a long competition you would have more carbohydrate energy left over later in the competition that you didn't have before. IF you remem-

ber one thing about this section it should be that hockey is NOT an endurance sport so this research is not really applicable to you!

How your muscle uses carbs and fats as fuels...

When you sprint, the majority of the energy you need comes from carbs. This fuel can be turned into energy without the use of oxygen from breathing and is the most effective at making you speedy in a sprint. Most sports will involve a sprint at some point so being carb-free will hurt most who are looking for a top performance.

When you move for longer than about 4 minutes, the oxygen system starts producing the majority of the energy you need. Every breath you breathe can help get oxygen to your muscles where the oxygen system uses a combination of carbs again and fat. Fat is only able to be used in the oxygen system. And, carbs are a preferred fuel over fat when oxygen is in short supply. Carbs gives you more "bang for your oxygen buck". So you should be looking for strategies that keep you full of carbs for longer during an endurance event when you could conceivably run out of carbs.

DIG DEEPER 8: UNDERSTANDING THE NUTRITION FACTS LABEL

Be smart and informed about what you put in your mouth. Be a label reader!

INFORMATION ON THE LABEL & WHAT THIS MEANS TO YOU

THE INGREDIENT LIST

Ingredients are listed in order of weight, from most to least. This means that the food contains more of the ingredients at the beginning of the list than at the end of the list. This can help you to compare foods. A bread that lists "whole wheat flour" first is less processed than one that lists "enriched flour" first. Look for ingredients that are less processed.

THE PORTION SIZE

The quantities listed on the label are all based on a specific amount of food or drink. Often the label portion is less than what you end up eating. For example, a label might say one portion of cereal is 3/4 of a cup (185ml). The next time you eat cereal try measuring 3/4 of a cup (185ml) of cereal. Do you eat more? Make sure you multiply the numbers on the rest of the label to match your portion size. This takes some math!

THE PER CENT (%) OF DAILY VALUE

A good rule of thumb of Daily Values (DV) is 5% is a little bit and 15% is a lot. Some nutrients that you want LESS of are sugar, sodium, and trans fats. Some nutrients that you probably want MORE of are fibre, calcium and iron. The % DV should only be used to compare products. If soup A has 50% DV of sodium and soup B has 10% in the same size portion, it would be better to choose soup B, since most people consume WAY too much sodium.

Don't fall into the trap of buying fruit drinks or fruit cocktails instead of fruit juices because they say 100% vitamin C on the label. This does not mean that they are good for you. Compare the ingredient list of a fruit drink vs a fruit juice. We bet that you will never look at fruit drinks and cocktails the same way again!

FATS

Fat-free products or low fat products are not better for you. Some foods that have "fat-free" or "low fat" on their labels are really high in sugar. Check the Ingredient List and the Nutrition Facts label to see if there is something else in the product that you should watch out for. While fat needs to be consumed every day for energy, most people are eating too much processed fats in the form of oil and not enough whole food fats for example, seeds, nuts, and avocados. A good number to know for fats is 5. Every 5 grams of fat is equivalent to eating 1 teaspoon of oil. So, a food with 15 grams of fat has the equivalent of 3 teaspoons of oil in it. A diet low in polyunsaturated fats (found in fish oil, seeds and nuts) and high in trans fats (found in margarines and some baked goods) have been linked to disease, so try to eat foods with more polyunsaturated fats. The key word there is foods rather than products.

SODIUM

Athletes should be aware that sodium affects fluid balance in the body. Eating really salty foods will make you thirstier later on. This is great after a sweaty practice but it could be imbalancing at a pre-game meal. Most unprocessed foods will be naturally low in sodium. There is no set number of sodium to recommend for every athlete. Some may benefit from consuming less than 400 mg of sodium at all times and some may need 1000 mg or more after a very sweaty and long training session.

CARBOHYDRATES

The carbohydrate value is the most important nutrient for hockey players to check on the label. Carbohydrates can be eaten in the form of starch, fibre, or sugar. Total carbohydrate is the sum of starch + sugar + fibre. Carbohydrates are so important to hockey players that

there are two numbers to keep in mind. Number 5 for sugar. Every 5 grams of sugar is equivalent to a single sugar packet. Sugar can be used during sport to improve performance, but be careful not to overdo it at other times in the day. High sugar intake is directly linked to high body fat and poor concentration. How many sugar packets are in a single serving of your favourite cereal? Number 30 is for total carbohydrate. Every 30 grams of carbohydrate is equivalent to 2 slices of bread. How much bread do you like to eat before hockey? Eating foods high in carbohydrates but low in sugar is not a guarantee you are eating a less processed food. Here's a fun fact: White bread (which is low in sugar) will turn into sugar pretty much in your mouth. So eating white bread is like eating sugar. Eating 30 grams of carbohydrate in white bread is like eating 6 sugar packs!

PROTEIN

Once you know where you can get protein in foods, you can probably predict if a product has protein in it just by reading the ingredients. A good number to know for protein is 16. Every 16 grams of protein is equivalent to 2 eggs. Most young athletes will not need to eat more than 16 grams of protein in 1 sitting.

DIG DEEPER 9: HELPFUL RESOURCES

The Internet can be a tricky place to look for information. Here is a list of trusted websites that are Nutrition Edge approved!

Here's where to get more information on...

HOCKEY NUTRITION

www.eatthisforperformance.com/hockey

SUPPLEMENTS

www.ausport.gov.au/ais/nutrition

- The Australian Institute of Sport Nutrition delivers a world-class sports nutrition service to AIS sports and national teams.

www.nsf.org

- The NSF International organization gives products a certification that they contain what they say they contain. The NSF certification is useful to have on a product if an athlete will possibly be getting tested for illegal substances.

www.informed-choice.org

- Like NSF, the Informed-Choice organization gives a supplement a certification that it is free from prohibited substances.

EATING DISORDERS

www.nedic.ca

- National Eating Disorder Information Centre

GENERAL NUTRITION

www.dietitians.ca

- Find a Canadian Dietitian near you and see what nutrition topics are important to Canadians.

www.eatright.org

- The Academy of Nutrition and Dietetics is the world's largest organization of food and nutrition professionals. This is an interesting website to go to if you want to know more about nutrition in general.

www.supertracker.usda.gov

- The United States Department of Agriculture has a great website that includes a "Food-A-Pedia" section which allows you to find out the nutrition information for over 8000 foods!

www.extenso.org

- (in French) Université de Montréal's nutrition reference center

ENVIRONMENTAL

www.seachoice.org

- This organization lists which fish are the best to eat for sustain ability of the fishing industry and for your health.

PROFESSIONAL REFERENCES

All professional references used in this book can be found on the Eat This for Performance website.

Made in the USA
Lexington, KY
18 April 2019